THE SWIRL AND SWING OF WORDS

EMBRACING THE WRITING LIFE

MEREDITH ALLARD

The Swirl and Swing of Words: Embracing the Writing Life

Lemon Moon Books

Cover design by Anne Rae Smith

ISBN: 979-8-218-54029-6

The Swirl and Swing of Words: Embracing the Writing Life/Meredith Allard – 1st paperback edition 2024

{1. Nonfiction. 2. Creative Writing—Nonfiction. 3. Writing Reference Creativity—Nonfiction. 4. Authorship—Nonfiction. 5. Creativity Self-Help —Nonfiction.} I. Title

I love writing. I love the swirl and swing of words as they tangle with human emotions.

—James Michener

INTRODUCTION

First forget inspiration. Habit is more dependable. Habit will sustain you whether you're inspired or not. Habit will help you finish and polish your stories. Inspiration won't. Habit is persistence in practice.

—Octavia E. Butler

They say that you teach what you need to learn. At least, that has been my experience writing this book. As with my previous nonfiction book, *Painting the Past: A Guide For Writing Historical Fiction*, I've been kicking around the idea for *The Swirl and Swing of Words* for some time.

I've considered myself a writer since the sixth grade when my teacher asked me to write the class graduation play. I think the request had more to do with my neat handwriting than any precocious writing skills I might have shown at age 11, but you take what you can get.

I was one of the lucky ones. Throughout elementary, middle, and high school I had teachers who took a moment to tell me that I was a good writer; as a result, I began to believe that I was a good writer. If you hear anything enough, good or bad, you begin to believe it. Since high school, after encouragement from my American Literature teacher, I had it in my head that I should become a writer. After a few hits and misses, I found my calling in writing novels, primarily historical fiction.

One of the most important lessons I've learned is that a creative life is an ebb and flow. Creativity can present you with the most miraculous highs. Other times, not so much. Like other writers, I had trouble finding my creativity at the beginning of the COVID epidemic. While I'm a homebody who is happiest at home with my books, my cats, and my writing, the strangeness of living in a shut-down world made creativity harder to access. I know other writers suffered the same. In her book *Writing On Empty*, Natalie Goldberg said about her own difficulties during the lockdowns: "I didn't want to be a writer anymore. I didn't want to teach writing. But when I stopped both, a chasm opened. Endless forms of suffering slapped me in the face." I felt the same. Writing—the one thing that has always given my life a sense of purpose—became a chore I couldn't force myself to do. While I had trouble finding the headspace to be creative, I felt a lack within me, with a widening void following close behind.

During that time, I read a lot. I journaled, I colored in coloring books, and I painted in my art journal. I started doing yoga again, and I started meditating after a too-long break. I cooked, I baked, I watched TV, I sat on my patio watching the sunset, and I drank too much coffee and tea. I was learning how to be in the moment, which is something I've never been particularly good at. I watched YouTube videos about slow living and realized, hey, that's what I'm doing! I'm living quietly, taking each day at a time, learning to appreciate this moment instead of staying lost in the past or worrying about the future. It sounds easy, doesn't it? To appreciate the moment we're in? Anyone who has ever tried it knows that it's a lifelong practice to learn how to appreciate every moment for what it is—a gift.

Like most creative people, I've had several brushes with burnout over the years. Although writing can be hard, I love it. Like James Michener, I love the swirl and swing of words. I love the challenge and the puzzle of making them do my bidding. When I write, I feel most at home in my skin. I feel as if I'm doing what I was put here to do. Writing has saved my life more often than I can count. From the time when I was a teenager journaling my family-filled angst into spiral notebooks, writing has been my way of making sense of my life. Writing allows me to connect with others when there seems to be no other way to bridge that gap. John Green said, "Writing is something you do alone. It's a profession for introverts who want to tell you a story but don't want to make eye contact while doing it." I love telling stories above all else, and creative writing allows me to tap into my imagination in limitless ways.

I thought it would be helpful for me to share my experiences with embracing the writing life. As the kids say, your mileage will vary. I hope other writers will recognize some of themselves in the joys and struggles that come with choosing a creative life. While writing itself is a solitary activity, we are not alone in our dreams, concerns, and backaches. When we accept writing for what it is—one of the best things we can do for ourselves—then we can embrace it with all that we have to give.

As with my previous nonfiction book, this book isn't about selling as many books as you can, writing 15000 words a day, or marketing anything. This book is about sharing a deep, abiding love for writing, a love that has sustained me through many storms. This book is about how I came to embrace the writing life over trials and errors, ups and downs, experiments and, finally, acceptance of my creative life how it is and not how I wish it to be. Writing this book has helped me clarify my experience with living an authentic creative life in this precious time we have. Perhaps you would like to do the same.

1

LEANING IN

What are you willing to give up in order to become who you really need to be?
—Elizabeth Gilbert

WRITERS ARE LIKE ANYONE ELSE. We require shelter, food, and water. We need companionship, in human or animal form. We do better if we recognize our purpose in this world. For me, that purpose is writing.

I'm not sure that being a writer or embracing the writing life are the same things. We can be writers without pining for the writing life. Placing words on the page isn't always a creative act, though it is for me and most writers I know. For some people, writing is their business and that's all it is to them. For me, writing is the lens through which I see this crazy world. My identity is largely connected with being a writer. While I'm talking specifically about writing, you can fill in the blank with any artistic endeavor. Perhaps you pine for the painting life in the same way that I pine for the writing life, which is to say that I seek to embrace every ounce of creativity offered to me.

I should begin by saying what I think the writing life *isn't.* A writing life doesn't mean you have to write all day. It doesn't mean you have to write every day. It certainly doesn't mean you have to make your living writing. Most writers don't make a living writing. Some do, but most don't. Being a writer doesn't mean that you have to be an alcoholic or a starving artist. You can pay your bills, eat regularly, and write just fine.

So what, then, is the writing life?

The writing life is making a commitment to putting words on paper, whether by hand or by keyboard. It means staying in close contact with the storyteller inside you. It means being attuned to the inspiration all around you. It means rediscovering your inner child—the one who loved to play make-believe, dress in costumes, and create worlds under homemade tents. It means remembering the activities you loved when you were younger and probably still do deep down somewhere, buried beneath grocery lists and unpaid bills.

The writing life means freely admitting your love of language, rhythm, and story. The writing life is born from a love of words—first in relentlessly pursuing other people's words and then in pursuing our own. The writing life means seeking beauty in the everyday that others, who are not artists, might consider mundane. For me, sitting on my shady patio in the cooler morning air, especially on so-hot desert summer days, enjoying the green of the plants surrounding me, drinking a cup of tea, watching the trees, and seeing the valley in the distance is a perfect morning. I can listen to the birds sing and simply be. That is a moment of true beauty.

While it doesn't seem like sitting outside should have anything to do with writing, it has a lot to do with writing because it's those little moments of contemplation that help to fill our creative wells. Think of a water well. Those wells could be full, overflowing, or they could run dry. It's the same with creativity. Sometimes, our creative wells are full. We dip our bucket down and plenty of thoughts, inspirations, and visions rise to the surface. Other times, our creative wells run dry and our buckets come up empty. Leaning into the writing life allows me to refill that creative well. For some of us, leaning into the writing life means accepting who we are at face value and using our unique perspectives as a strength instead of a weakness.

Henry David Thoreau said, "I went to the woods because I wished to live deliberately, to front only the essential facts of life, and see if I could not learn what it had to teach, and not, when I came to die, discover that I had not lived." For me, living deliberately means accepting that I'm not a complete person unless I give these stories breathing fire within me free range. For some of us, writing is our calling, so embracing the writing life means discovering that calling, acknowledging it, and staying true to it despite the myriad of challenges we face every day. Embracing the writing life means tapping into our creativity, letting our souls roam free, and sharing the truest part of ourselves. Often, it means that we go against the grain in how we choose to live because predetermined expectations don't work for us.

I've certainly experienced down times when writing has felt like a chore, as if it were something I did because I expected it of myself. Lawrence Kasdan said, "Being a writer is like having homework every day." There have been times when I grew tired of the homework and lost the joy that writing had always brought me. I forgot how much fun it was to write a story for the story's sake, because I got to spend time in a world that I created. I mourned the loss of that joy, and I wondered how to get it back. What is the point of writing if you don't enjoy it?

You may be familiar with the Zen term *shoshin*, which is translated as beginner's mind. Here's a wonderful definition of beginner's mind from Leo Babauta from the website Zen Habits: "If you've ever learned something new, you can remember what that's like: you're confused because you don't know how to do whatever you're learning, but you're also looking at everything as if it's brand new, perhaps with curiosity and wonder." I had lost my curiosity and wonder. I had lost my beginner's mind. My goal then was to reclaim it. Embracing the writing life takes effort. It requires persistence.

For me, living deliberately includes making space for writing. I'm not writing because I *have* to, because it's that dreaded homework. I'm writing because I *want* to. Because it's an authentic part of who I am. Because it makes me happy. Because it brings me peace. When I talk about writing, I'm talking about the act of world-building and storytelling, but I also mean the physical act—sitting my bottom into the chair and dancing my fingers across the keyboard, typing out words that become sentences that, in time, become essays or novels. Toni Morrison said, "But writing was the real freedom because nobody told me what to do there. That was my world and my imagination. And all my life it's been that way, even now." The freedom writing gives me is palpable. When all else fails me, as it sometimes does, writing saves me.

Whether you love to write, or if you have some other creative endeavor that lights you up from the inside, your time may feel fuller when you decide to include the magic of creativity. Writing is how I suck the marrow out of life. "Writing is the act of reaching across the abyss of isolation to share and reflect," said Natalie Goldberg. And it should be writing spurred by joy. By leaning into my creativity, I've found that joy again.

As Elizabeth Gilbert asks, what are you willing to give up in order to become who you really need to be? Are you willing to give up wasting time living according to other people's expectations? According to preconceived ideas about what your life should look like? Your own outdated vision of yourself in five years, ten years, at the end of your life? It takes a lifetime to accept ourselves for who we are. It's a journey I'm still on. Leaning into a creative life is a process, and it's a challenge I've finally embraced.

2

DEFINING SUCCESS

Popular success is a poor barometer of work and worth. In order for a work to connect commercially, stars must align and none of them relate to how good a project is. It might be the timing, the distribution mechanism, the mood of the culture, or a connection to current events.

—Rick Rubin

WE TEND to define our achievements according to popular success. As Rick Rubin said, there are often factors beyond our control that determine how commercially successful a creative work will be. I've learned to focus on the factor of success I have control over, and the only things I have true control over are the books I publish.

My most successful books have been the *Loving Husband Trilogy*, a paranormal fantasy about a vampire living in a human world. *Her Dear & Loving Husband*, the first book in the trilogy, was published in 2011 at the height of vampire fever. After the final book in the trilogy was published in 2013, I could have left my job because I was making enough money from book sales. The books I've published since then haven't been as successful, at least not monetarily. Does that mean those books are failures? Not at all. It just means that they didn't hit the cultural zeitgeist like the *Loving Husband Trilogy* did.

When I started writing, I thought success meant making a million dollars and having my books turned into films. While I would never turn down a million dollars or a chance to see my stories on the screen, I've learned that success isn't always what it seems. In traditional publishing, most author advances are between $5000 and $10000. Independent authors have to pay for book cover design and editing before their books are released. With time and experience, I've realized that making a million dollars from my books isn't likely to happen. As a result, I had to redefine what success meant for me. I decided that, while the huge bestseller wasn't likely to happen, perhaps I could make a living from writing. I don't need a million dollars to live comfortably. Making as much as my salary at my job would be adequate.

We've all heard that quote about how we should enjoy the journey instead of the destination. I was so focused on my destination, making a living as a writer, that I forgot to enjoy the journey. When making a living as a writer became fraught with expectations, it sapped my creative bliss to the point where I thought I would never love writing again. I had convinced myself that I wanted to make a living as a writer, but the things I needed to do to make that happen didn't align with how I wanted to spend my time.

I had to accept the truth about the type of books I wanted to write. If you read those "How to publish" articles, often they state the obvious: the books that sell the most are genre fiction, such as romance, fantasy, mystery, thrillers, and science fiction. Some authors who sell a lot of books write to market, meaning that they see what genres or sub-genres are hot; they write books in those genres, and they publish their books as quickly as they can. There's nothing wrong with writing to market if that's what you enjoy doing.

When I was at university, one of my fellow students wrote romances for Harlequin, and she told me I should give it a go. My classmate was in her 50s, with long yellow-gray hair. She wore flannel shirts over rock band t-shirts, faded blue jeans, and Doc Martin boots. She was a chain smoker, which you could smell at a close distance as well as hear in her gravelly voice. She said that she and her husband wrote the books together. They were able to write quickly, and they made a solid income. I've come back to her advice over the years. There have been times when I decided, "I'll write romances since they sell well. Then the money I make writing romances will finance my literary novels."

Many authors do just that and it works well for them. For some reason, I'm unable to force myself to write something I'm not compelled to write. One time, I settled my mind to writing a romance and I got as far as page 12 before I abandoned the project. I wasn't interested enough to make myself write it. I love that quote from Toni Morrison, "If there is a book you want to read and it has not been written, then you must write it." But the opposite is also true. If there is a book I don't want to read, then I shouldn't be the one to write it. There are so many talented romance authors who love the genre and have huge followings who buy their new releases as soon as they become available. Authors who love to read romance are the ones who should be writing romance.

So...if I don't write the kind of books that sell a lot, then what?

When I began writing *Her Dear & Loving Husband*, my initial idea was to write a paranormal romance about a vampire who finds his one true love. Once I started writing, the story evolved into a hybrid of literary fiction, historical fiction, and paranormal fantasy that examines the good and bad of human nature. When I had *Her Dear & Loving Husband* critiqued, the beta reader, who was a romance novelist, suggested I turn it into a traditional romance by adding some steamy sexy-time scenes and deleting the literary flights of fancy. She wanted me to turn my main character, James Wentworth, into an alpha male. I thought long and hard about whether or not I should follow her advice, even though such changes would alter the fabric of the story. I was tempted to do it. Finally, I realized that the book she suggested was not the book my heart wanted to write. I decided to write the novel the way I envisioned it, not the novel that would fit more easily into a genre. I knew my artistic choices could cost me readers, but after a lot of consideration, I decided I was all right with that. Success for me no longer came in the form of huge numbers (though I won't argue with huge numbers if they happen) or even in making a living as a writer. I believed that if I wrote the book I needed to write, readers would relate to it on that level. I believed there was an audience for my *Loving Husband* stories. Luckily, I was right. Book Three in the series, *Her Loving Husband's Return*, landed on the Amazon best seller list the day it was released when I had done exactly zero things to promote it. Is that success? It is to me.

I'm proud of every book I've published even though some have been more financially successful than others. Some of my books I've never quite figured out how to market since I'm not entirely sure what the book is, except that the story wouldn't let me go until I wrote it down and set it free. I prefer to follow my imagination wherever it takes me. If you love writing anything and everything, then do whatever is right for you. The joy of embracing the writing life means that we get to decide for ourselves what works and what doesn't.

One interesting fact I've noticed over the years is how, whenever the topic turns to writers who write as an artistic pursuit, someone takes offense and says, "Why can't I write for money? Why do I have to defend myself because I want to make money writing?" You don't have to defend yourself. If you want to write for money, then write for money. No one is naysaying that idea, especially not me. But if I write because I wish to share my stories the way I see them, then I can make that choice too.

Actually, I think it's the other way around. If anything, those of us who write for artistic expression are the ones who feel the need to defend ourselves because we're not focused on the same things as everyone else. And let's face it —it can be scary when you make your own way instead of following the pack.

Just as I had to find my own road as an author, I had to find my own road as a publisher. If I hear about a marketing tip that sounds reasonable, then I'll try it. I'll try anything once, leaving my marketing strategy as a kind of throwing spaghetti at the wall to see what sticks. I learn about marketing, I experiment, and I see what works for me. That's what this is—a grand experimental recipe, and each of us has to find our own ingredients for success.

There will never be a one-size-fits-all solution for publishing or marketing. We've written different books that appeal to different audiences. We have different personalities and different ways we like to connect with people. The best advice I can offer, if I should be offering advice, is to read whatever you can find from other authors who have been there and done that. Weed out the helpful information from the not-so-helpful since all advice isn't created equal. How do you know what's sound advice and what isn't? I like the tried-and-true method of "If it sounds too good to be true, it probably is." There is a lot of good free advice out there. There is also some bad free advice. I'm not a fan of marketing advice that says, "Do it my way or your book will dissolve into thin air!" What works for one author may not work for you, but you don't know until you try.

Once I learned to look at marketing as an experiment, I learned to have fun with it. I didn't need to drive myself to distraction searching for some hidden gem of knowledge. What I need is to discover and grow. There's always something new to learn, and there's no time limit. That's one of the great things about publishing these days—there's no longer a shelf life on books. We can continue to find new readers as long as we're willing to give it our time and attention.

How do I define success now? I define success as having readers in the world who love my books and look forward to my next release. The success of the *Loving Husband Trilogy* was amazing, especially in hindsight since I knew next to nothing about marketing and didn't spend a lot of money to publicize the book. The success was largely due to word of mouth, which is always the best publicity. I don't have the largest audience in the world, but I have loyal readers, and I'm thankful for every one of them. I've learned to take my hard-won writing career, hold onto it with both hands, and never let it go.

Success also means being proud of the work I publish.

My definition of success may be different from others, and that's okay. Success means listening to my heart because my heart knows the right thing to do. Success means letting go of the idea that the only success is material in nature. Simply completing the work is success since so many people who want to write books begin the journey but never finish. Conquering the fear is success beyond measure.

Suffering is the difference between how life is and how we wish it to be. By accepting things as they are, I allow myself an artistic freedom that I might not have otherwise. It's only through artistic freedom that I'm able to make bona fide creative decisions that are mine alone. For me, that is success.

3

HOW DO YOU MAKE A LIVING?

You will never be able to escape your heart. So it is better to listen to what it has to say.

—Paolo Coelho

IT TOOK me years to accept the fact that I prefer having a steady paycheck that comes twice a month instead of depending on the unreliability of book sales, a creative business, or freelance work. Even the most successful creatives have good and bad months. Some months, the work sells well, and some months, it's as if no one knows we exist.

Every writing podcast and website is devoted to telling people how to leave behind the dreadful day job (Bad job! Bad job!) and make a living writing or running a creative business. It doesn't surprise me that quitting the day job is the focus for so many authors. It was my goal for a long time too. We tend to judge things by their dollar value (or pound value, or yen value, or whatever you use where you live). The general belief is that when you quit your day job because you make enough money selling books, then and only then have you conquered that elusive mountain called Success, leaving the rest of us to dream of the Success that eludes us.

There are a lot of authors out there—both traditional and independent—who are doing brilliantly with their books. They're making a lot of money, and some of them do leave their jobs. Most authors want to sell as many books as they can. I certainly do. However, like with everything else in life, it's important for each of us to decide for ourselves what we *really* want, not what we're told to want by others. For a long time, I felt like a failure for holding onto my day job. "I need to be brave and quit," I kept telling myself. Just do it! I finally had to accept that what I *really* want is financial security. For me, financial security means having enough to pay my rent and my bills, put gas in my car, go grocery shopping, and have savings set aside, you know, usual life stuff. I love the idea of making a living from my books, but I also love knowing that I can eat whether I have a good sales month or not.

Blame it on my childhood. I do. I love Charles Dickens for his wonderful storytelling, but my attachment to him also stems from the similarities in our early lives. Dickens' father, John, spent money faster than he made it, ending up in a debtors' prison when Dickens was 12. While I was never sent to work in a blacking factory like Dickens (that I recall), I, too, was raised by parents who never grew up when it came to money.

My parents were 16 and 20 when they met, and two kids later, they remained teenagers in the lack of maturity they displayed when it came to financial matters. If there were debtors' prisons in the 1980s, the Allards would have been permanent residents. There was never enough money. My father was fired from every job he ever had for reasons ranging from being late to stealing money to stealing goods from the automobile parts departments where he worked. My mother worked occasionally, part-time jobs here and there, but mainly she spent her time screaming at my father for not being able to hold a job. While my parents were engaged in Olympic-level yelling matches, my brother gave more than his fair share of verbal abuse while busting his fist through his bedroom wall when he didn't get his way. Sounds fun, right?

We were evicted from every place we ever lived. The electricity was turned off too many times to count. There were mornings when we'd go outside for my mother to drive my brother and me to school and the car wasn't there, vanished to Repo Man Heaven. I remember a family friend sending my mother home with bags of groceries because there wasn't enough money for food. I don't remember being hungry, but I do remember the sickening feeling that comes with moneylessness. I decided at a young age that that was never going to be me, and it never has been. Since I've been an adult and responsible for my own life, I've made decisions that allow me to make sure that I have enough money to take care of myself. Mind you, I'm a high school English teacher, so I'm not bringing in the big bucks here. But I live beneath my means, which means that I know my rent and my bills will be paid, and I have savings. For someone who grew up in poverty, the peace of mind that comes with having enough money to live comfortably has a price beyond measure.

Still, there have been times when I wanted to be my own boss. About ten years ago, I thought I'd give freelance writing a try. I hated freelance writing. I mean, I hated it. I hated that even though I always submitted my work before the deadline, the magazines or websites paid me when they got around to it. Sometimes the payment wasn't the right amount (Did we agree to $400? I have here $250...), and sometimes my payment was lost in transit (Are you sure you didn't get it? It says here it was deposited last Tuesday...). Sometimes, there wasn't as much work in July as there was in May, and I felt like a child again, worrying about whether or not the bills would be paid.

I know writers want to make a living writing, but the reality is that few do. The thing about book sales is that they fluctuate. After a while, sales of even best-selling books slow down. If you make enough money while sales are hot to feel confident depending on that as your income, then do so. If you have a more adventurous spirit than I do, then do what feels right for you. I'm simply showing why leaving our jobs isn't the ultimate goal for every creative person in the world. Book sales are part of the ebb and flow of life. Sometimes books sell well, sometimes they don't. Sometimes you feel like a nut, sometimes you don't.

If I had depended on the sales of the *Loving Husband Trilogy* as my sole income, I would have done well for about a year, but then what would I have done when sales slowed down? Common wisdom says to write more books so readers have more to buy from you. When I'm being true to my creative process, I publish one book a year, which isn't fast enough to keep the momentum going. Writers who publish quickly often end up burning out because they can't keep up with the frantic pace; even if they do keep up, there's no guarantee that every book will sell as well as previous books. There's too much we don't have control over when it comes to book sales. For me, book sales provide a second income. I don't have the stress of worrying about sales or trying to go viral on social media since I have a steady paycheck. After I do what I can, the books sell what they sell. I've learned to become zen about the whole book sales thing. My life is a lot less stressful that way.

We write books because we want people to read them, and book sales are a good indicator of how many people are reading our books. Beyond that, I suspect that people want to leave their jobs for other reasons. We saw inklings of this during the COVID years when the Great Resignation hit and people were leaving their jobs in droves. Then, when people realized they still needed a roof over their heads, we went from the Great Resignation to Quiet Quitting, where people kept their jobs but kept the amount of work they did to a bare minimum. I wonder if the issue is less that people feel as if they must make their living as writers and more that they are unhappy with their current jobs and think making a living selling books would make them happier.

If you ask long-time writers, most would say that writing is not going to be a get-rich-quick scheme. Yes, there are a few authors who hit it big with their first books, but they are the outliers. The majority of authors need to write for years before they can craft something others are excited to read. Even if you have a loyal following, there are no guarantees about how many books you're going to sell. In that case, you'll need another source of income. As Chuck Wendig said, "There is zero shame in a day job. Part-time, full-time, whatever. And a day job may very well be crucial because writing—as a hobby, as a semi-pro endeavor, or as a full professional gig—is not always a delivery system for reliable income."

The general wisdom is to commodify everything. We've done our creativity a great injustice by insisting that the only way to be successful is to make a boatload of money at it. Whenever someone shows the tiniest aptitude at something, we tell them to make money from it. If you enjoy baking, you should open a bakery. If you like writing, you should make a living selling your books. Find your passion and make money at it! The problem with this way of thinking is that it forgets that we need people with jobs in our society. We need doctors and nurses and teachers and car mechanics and people who know how to fix things. I'm sure being a trash collector isn't the most exciting job in the world, and I'm pretty sure it's no one's passion, but I certainly don't want to live someplace where the trash isn't collected. In *The Creative Act*, Rick Rubin said, "...if the choice is between making great art and supporting yourself, the art comes first. Consider another way to make a living. Success is harder to come by when your life depends on it."

The novelist Octavia E. Butler worked as a telemarketer. She also worked as a warehouse worker, a dishwasher, and a potato chip inspector. Although potato chip inspector sounds kind of cool. I would be a potato chip inspector. Rick Rubin calls work like this, "jobs that demand your time, but little else." Butler was university-educated, but she chose low-wage jobs so that she would have time for writing. She woke up at 2 a.m. so she could write before the day's work. Butler is rightfully known as one of the queens of science fiction and fantasy. I read her time-travel novel *Kindred* while I was writing my own time-travel story, and her storytelling skills blew me away. Perhaps, for those of us who want to put our creativity first, we might choose a job that takes up our time and little else, thereby reserving our mental space for our creative endeavors.

We should pursue our goals unreservedly. We should discover our passions, plant them, water them, cultivate them, and watch them bloom. But as Elizabeth Gilbert said in *Big Magic*, we are doing our creativity a great injustice by expecting it to make our living for us. Rick Rubin said much the same. I've lost track of the number of times I've heard creatives say that making money with their passion takes the joy away since what was once a fulfilling form of self-exploration and self-expression became something to panic over. In such cases, their passion became a job, complete with all of the stresses and frustrations they were trying to leave behind in the first place.

Professor Erin Cech said, "Passion shouldn't be the standard to which everyone is held when we're asking them what they do for work...We have to recognize that people have different motivations for why they work hard." I can be more creative because I don't have to worry about how I'm going to make ends meet, even during those months when my book sales are slow. Yes, I have less time to write than I would if I quit my job, but you know what? The writing gets done. One of my favorite authors is Abraham Verghese, who is a medical doctor and a professor at Stanford. It took him 14 years to write *The Covenant of Water* while he continued both of his busy jobs. Yes, it took him 14 years to write his novel but look at what he had at the end—a modern masterpiece.

Many writers, sometimes even the most respected and beloved authors, don't make as much money writing as we think they do. In *Bird By Bird*, Anne Lamott shares how she struggled financially at the beginning of her writing career, and she's *Anne Freakin' Lamott*—the goddess of all things writing. My main man Dickens also struggled financially for a good portion of his career, and he's *Charles Freakin' Dickens*. He complained he was cheated by his publishers—sound familiar?—while he tried to raise his large family in

London, which was too expensive even in the Victorian era. Dickens didn't do well financially until he began his reading engagements where he acted out scenes from his novels to enraptured audiences. Some scholars say that the exhaustion from the readings destroyed his health and ultimately killed him, so maybe that's not the best example. My point, and I do have one, is that even the best writers don't always make a living from book sales.

These days, there are other ways for creatives to make money. You can have a podcast, a vlog, and a blog. You can also go on speaking engagements and create courses to sell online. If those endeavors sound interesting to you, then try them out. I tried creating a podcast when I was running *The Copperfield Review,* and by the third week I realized that I didn't enjoy it. I didn't find the process of running a podcast interesting enough to sustain, and it took too much time away from writing. I want to write, not research, record, and edit podcasts. I'm a homebody, and the idea of traveling to speaking engagements doesn't thrill me either. A steady paycheck allows me the time and the mental space to write instead of doing things that aren't interesting to me. For a while, I worked as a freelance editor who helped writers with their historical novel manuscripts. When the work lost its luster, I was able to let it go and focus on my own writing. I can write my books, market them to the best of my ability, and then I can relax knowing that my rent will be paid and whatever books I sell will be extra income. A job is not an excuse for not writing. If you're an artist, the art will happen. That's what makes you an artist.

It might sound counterintuitive to say that to embrace the writing life you don't need to make a living writing, but it isn't really. Embracing the writing life is about being true to who you are and what you want from your art. Having a job means that I'm free to create in a way that allows my unique author's voice to soar without worries that my books won't sell enough. Whether I have a good sales month or a not-as-good sales month, I'll have a roof over my head and I'll be able to eat, which are both very good things.

4

CREATIVE RHYTHMS

 *writer is a person for whom writing is more difficult than it is for other people.*

—Thomas Mann

As much as I love writing, my creativity ebbs and flows as my circumstances change. My creative energy wavers depending on whatever life stuff I'm dealing with at any given moment. While it's true that writing gives me energy because I'm tapping into the truest part of myself, writing also depletes my energy since it's not easy to find the right words to express what I'm trying to say.

Productivity is something I've given a lot of thought to over the years. We've all become so geared toward doing more, achieving more, and producing more that we forget to be honest with ourselves about what we want. As Natalie Goldberg said, "No matter your age there is a sense of urgency, to make life immediate and relevant." Most of us begin our writing lives with certain self-imposed expectations. I will write this many words a day. I will publish this many books a year. I will win this many awards and appear on this many bestseller lists. I will exorcise my demons. I will be seen, heard, and appreciated, perhaps for the first time. I will make this much money. When I do, my life will be perfect. Then reality steps in and we think we should be doing more, and more, and even more after that.

It wasn't long ago that productivity was all the rage. It's still a popular topic. Everyone declared themselves an expert on how to get more work done, and many of us, including myself, followed their didactic prescriptions about how to squeeze the most out of every day. You're not serious about achieving your dreams if you're not working toward it every possible minute, the experts insisted. And I believed them. If I wasn't doing something that had to do with my writing, then I felt that moment slipping away, forever unused.

Writers have heard all of the usual productivity standbys: You must write every day! You must write thousands of words at a time! You must publish a book every two months! You must write in the genres that sell the most books! You must, you must, you must!

Heavens.

These days, we see posts about setting mini-goals or reasonable goals. That's more like it. After all, how can a stranger know my life, my responsibilities, my choices, or the out-of-my-control instances I'm dealing with at any given moment? I realized that it was up to me to find my own rhythm in this world.

If we have a dream we want to achieve, then we must set time aside to work toward that dream. If you want to write a book, then you work a little bit every day toward writing that book. Setting small, achievable goals should be the priority. In *Bird By Bird*, Anne Lamott refers to these small goals as short assignments. According to Lamott, we should focus on writing one scene at a time, something we can see through a one-inch picture frame. By writing that one scene, we've made progress, and that is the most important thing.

We should not work all day every day without a minute to spare for anything else. Feeling like we have to maximize the amount of work we get done in a prescribed amount of time only adds more stress to our already pushed-to-the-limit lives. We are writers, yes, but we are also doctors and teachers and office assistants and grocery store workers and clerks and parents and friends. Writing, while it's an important part of my life, is not the only part of my life, and I need to embrace all of who I am.

I didn't suffer as much as others during the COVID lockdowns, yet I still found my creative rhythm sidetracked. Then I had a wonky 2022 after I discovered that I was losing whatever was left of my hearing. I've never had much hearing in my right ear, and for most of my life I had a moderate loss in my left ear. Now, the hearing in my right ear has flatlined, and my left ear has deteriorated to a moderately severe loss. According to my audiologist, "We still have a few tones to work with," which are not the most encouraging words I've ever heard. When I saw one of the top ENTs in the Southern Nevada area, I asked him what happens when I can't hear well enough to function in the world. His answer was a shrug. I shrug at you, sir. I shrug at you. Beyond shrugging, the discovery was depressing. Suddenly, writing was the least important thing to me, which was odd since for most of my life writing was the only thing that mattered.

I mention this not for sympathy's sake. As my favorite cook, Mrs. Patmore, said, "Sympathy butters no parsnips." I'm sharing this because sometimes we need to let go of abstract ideas like "productivity" when such concepts aren't serving us. Sometimes, we need to be kind to ourselves while being honest about what we need. If we need a break, which I did desperately, then we need a break.

A sense of urgency can serve us well when we're engrossed in writing our stories, fiction or nonfiction. The need to share our inner worlds with others gives us the push to keep going when the work becomes difficult. But there are times when a sense of urgency can work against us by making us feel worthless or not up to the task because we're too overwhelmed by the curveballs life can throw at us. We all feel this way from time to time. No matter how much we love to create, there are times when we need to step away for our own sanity.

Not everything can be planned ahead. Not every minute of every day can be scheduled. Where is the joy of organic discovery if every moment has to conform to some preconceived idea of productivity? If giving yourself a writing sabbatical is useful, then you have permission to do that. Actually, you don't need permission. You get to do whatever is right for you because it's right for you. You don't need to explain yourself to anyone.

And then, when you're ready, you'll take baby steps to begin writing again.

5

THE MAGIC OF ORDINARY DAYS

Nowadays, people are so jeezled up. If they took some chamomile tea and spent more time rocking on the porch in the evening listening to the liquid song of the hermit thrush, they might enjoy life more.

—Tasha Tudor

IT'S NOT surprising that productivity is considered so important in our society. In our fast-paced culture, we're consistently besieged by advertisements, consumerism, social media, and every kind of content, as well as a push to maximize our time. As our attention jumps from here to there, we feel as if we're in a race with time.

No matter how much we feel we should be doing, there are still only 24 hours in a day. Which creative activities do we keep, which do we delay, and which do we send on their merry way? Thich Nhat Hanh said, "You've been running looking for something because you think that thing is crucial to your peace and happiness. You push yourself to achieve this and that condition so that you can be happy."

Hanh continued, "...the wonders of life are already here. They're calling you. If you can listen to them you will be able to stop running." Over time, I have learned to seek the magic in ordinary days.

I decided in 2023 to pursue a more deliberate life, as Thoreau beckons us to do. Seeking magic in ordinary days means paying attention to everything I do. Instead of always feeling like I need to have exciting experiences, I find joy in making tea and drinking it, feeling the comfort of the warm cup in my hands as I enjoy the scent of the bergamot oil. Seeking magic in ordinary days means living with intention as well as attention to the world around me: basking in the sweet fragrance of chocolate chip cookies as they bake, diving deeply into the worlds of the stories I read, sitting in the park enjoying the trees and the green.

Even shopping for produce can be a joy. There's a small farmer's market near my favorite coffee shop. The farmers come to Nevada from California and they sell organic produce that I love to mull over. I needed carrots for a recipe I cooked recently, and I took great joy in choosing from the purple, yellow, and orange organic carrots. Before, I would have grabbed whatever was handy at the supermarket. Now, even shopping for carrots can be a way to appreciate the moment.

Eating homemade food is a simple way to appreciate my health. I have a slow cooker, and while slow cookers are great for autumn and winter, they're also great for summer here in Southern Nevada, where the temperature, as I write this, is 119 degrees Fahrenheit and the sky is an ashy gray-blue from the wildfires sending smoke into the Las Vegas valley. The slow cooker allows me to cook easy, healthy meals that don't turn my entire house into an oven. Chopping vegetables and measuring spices—most people would find them to be mundane tasks, but I've come to find peace in the little things. This is simply another form of mindfulness that allows us to shift our perspectives in a way that allows us to view even the most ordinary tasks with gratitude. If we can turn the smallest moment into something beautiful, we can take joy where before we might have found annoyance or impatience.

Folding the laundry can become meditative if I allow it to be. Something as simple as opening the windows and letting fresh air and natural light into the room can be a wonderful moment, but you have to slow down enough to appreciate it. I lived in the Las Vegas area for several years before I realized what beautiful sunsets we have here. One night, I was driving home later than usual and I noticed how pretty the fading purple-pink sky was. Since then, I've learned to appreciate those sunsets on a nightly basis. Now, I live in the hills overlooking the valley, and every night I open my blinds and appreciate the pastel-painted horizon.

Being out in nature is one of the best ways to find magic in ordinary days. Feeling the warmth of the sun, seeing the flowers in bloom, watching the birds fly in graceful swirls, and watching the wind sweep through the desert landscape can be wonderful ways to experience natural beauty. Seeing the foliage change from green to red, orange, and yellow in the autumn and allowing the brisk air to wake you up in winter—there's little that can top that. Wherever you live, whatever the scenery, learn to see the beauty in it. Just as it took me years to appreciate the desert sunsets, it also took me years to appreciate the desert beauty, and now I love the red-rock canyons, the sprouts of green, and the bright-light sun. If you live near hiking, go for a walk, even a short one. If you live near pretty neighborhood parks as I do, then make a point of visiting as often as you can. Leave your electronic doo-dahs behind and allow yourself to take in the beauty around you. Allow nature to excite your senses. What do you see, hear, smell? Enjoy all of it.

You don't need to go to the park. I have a tiny patio outside my kitchen, and in the mornings on the weekends and days I'm not at work I make myself a cup of coffee and take my breakfast outside. I sit in a lawn chair surrounded by my potted plants, and I spend quiet time watching birds perch in the hanging tree and I listen to their songs. Bird-watching can be a joy. One day, I noticed funny-looking birds that looked like they were wearing black hats. What I saw were plumes, but at first glance the feathers looked like hats, so since then I have referred to Gambel's quails as "birds with funny hats." I have an app on my phone that allows me to take pictures of birds and plants and the app tells me what species they are. I've discovered rock pigeons, as well as kinglets and wrens. Poet Joy Harjo said, "Remember the plants, trees, animal life who all have their families, their histories too. Talk to them, listen to them. They are alive poems." How often do we go about our days without considering the living poetry of the natural world around us? I'm much happier bird-watching than other activities I used to do to keep myself occupied. Before COVID, I spent my Saturdays going from shop to shop, buying things I didn't need or even particularly want because that was how I had always spent my free hours. Now, I go out for coffee, I do my grocery shopping, and I come home and do things I want to do.

Learning to cut back on devices can also be a good thing. When I'm home, I drop my phone into my bag and I check it once a day. As soon as I heard that phones were designed to make people addicted so that we get dopamine hits the same way we do when we play slot machines, I lost interest.

I'd rather not have my brain rewritten, thank you. I'd rather spend my time baking, reading, or writing. I'd rather enjoy my time doing things I love, simple things, yes, but they're things that make me happy.

For writers, nothing is better than writing time. I don't mean that our writing time always needs to be spent working on a project, although projects are wonderful. Still, you don't have to limit yourself to writing to connect to your creativity. You can color, or you can art journal; really, anything you make with your hands can help you savor the moment. I'm learning how to crochet, which I'm still not very good at, but I'm learning to love the process. My one finished crochet project so far, a blanket, sits proudly over my chair. Every time I look at it I feel happy because I made it. Before, I wouldn't have taken the few months necessary for me to finish such a project. I would have become frustrated and I would have let the project go. I'm glad I stuck with it. There's nothing better than a homemade gift. Anyone can buy something from a shop, but not everyone is willing to take the time to make something. Simple scrapbooks of time spent together can be a wonderful gift, and it's something from your heart to theirs.

Be present in your life. Be grateful for what you have, even if you feel like you don't have enough. Many of us already have everything we need, but we're taught that it's not enough, or we're not enough, so we grasp for more. Then, when we get more, we're still not satisfied. Learning to be satisfied, even with a cup of tea, a good book, and time to spend being creative, is a great gift. When we seek the magic of ordinary days, we discover how to appreciate the creative journey. Tasha Tudor said, "There is no peace that cannot be found in the present moment."

A gratitude journal can be a wonderful way to connect

with the good things in your life. Most of my gratitude journal consists of entries about food and coffee. And books. And time to write. And cats. I have a lot of entries about cats. Focusing on the positive, especially when the world outside our windows seems to be going mad, can help us remember that things can get better over time. We can stay vigilant and still be positive.

Focus on your creativity. Focus on your writing. Be grateful for being a creative person because often we see the world not only as it is but as it can be. Creativity is a gift. Embrace that gift and nurture it. Rumi said, "The quieter we become, the more we can hear." Allow yourself to become so quiet that you can truly hear your life, perhaps for the first time. Your creativity will thank you.

If we can learn to be content with the magic of ordinary days like shimmering sunsets, if we can learn to let go of unrealistic expectations, if we can love writing for its own sake, then it's easier to find something to be grateful for. There are still good things, beautiful things in the world, even if we have to stretch to find them. Khalil Gibran said, "Keep your heart in wonder at the daily miracle of your life." There is wonder all around us if we dare to see it.

6

AN AUTHENTIC LIFE OR A FANTASY SELF?

Maybe the journey isn't so much about becoming anything. Maybe it's about un-becoming everything that isn't really you, so you can be who you were meant to be in the first place.

—Paolo Coelho

WHAT DOES it mean to live authentically? Many definitions of authentic living exist, but they all say basically the same thing: authentic living means living in a way that is true to the core of who you are. If you're a writer, it means living in a way that honors the writer in you. Brené Brown said, "Authenticity is the daily practice of letting go of who we think we're supposed to be and embracing who we are."

It's easy to conform to other people's expectations. A painter once told me how she disappointed her parents because she became an artist instead of a lawyer like they wanted. Art was central to her being, so she stayed true to her vision. To live authentically, we need to know who we are deep down, but few people take the time to examine their core beliefs; as a result, they don't know who they are deep down. They go through life doing what they think is expected of them and then can't figure out why they're unhappy. It's hard to be yourself in a society that demands conformity. We need to examine our beliefs, our strengths, our weaknesses, and our interests, even when they contradict what others expect of us. We should listen to our hearts instead of losing ourselves to external noise. We should know ourselves—both what we love to do and what we don't love to do. We need to own our truths and take responsibility for our choices.

Henry David Thoreau said, "We are constantly invited to be who we are." M. Scott Momaday said, "Our very existence consists in our imagination of ourselves. Our best destiny is to imagine, at least, completely, who and what and that we are. The greatest tragedy that can befall us is to go unimagined." To imagine ourselves, we must first give ourselves space to see our insides clearly. Is writing an authentic part of you? Do you feel, as I do, that you're only half yourself when you're not writing? There are so many excuses for not writing. There is so much resistance to allowing ourselves the imaginative freedom of a creative life. We feel as if we have to do everything for everyone else without considering our own well-being. Elizabeth Gilbert said, "A creative life is an amplified life. It's a bigger life, a happier life, an expanded life, and a hell of a lot more interesting life." But you have to choose to embrace that creative life.

It's easy to get trapped on the ceaseless treadmill of expectations heaped upon us by family, friends, even strangers on social media. To get off the treadmill means we have to be brave enough to listen to our hearts. Allow yourself to live a bigger, braver life. Walt Whitman said, "I contain multitudes." We all do. I embrace my multitudes by giving voice to the countless stories I want to share. I am all of my characters. I have lived their experiences. I have laughed at their jokes and cried at their misfortunes. I have lived many lives through my stories, and I hope to live many more. Only through writing am I able to express things I can't share any other way. Writing is when I'm my truest self.

Susan Cain, author of *Quiet*, said, "Spend your free time the way you like, not the way you think you're supposed to." What do you want to do with your free time? Do you want to write? Do you want to experience a creative life? We aren't guaranteed anything in this fragile existence. We aren't guaranteed health or wealth, happiness or time. Life is too short to waste following guidelines set by others who often don't have our best interests at heart. Dig in, find what you love, and do it.

The opposite of living an authentic life is engaging with a fantasy self. We all have fantasy selves. I certainly do. A fantasy self is the idealized life you wish you had but don't. Our fantasy selves are often some perfect versions of ourselves that we'll never be. A fantasy self is about how we perceive ourselves, but it's also about how others perceive us. We can be drawn to showcasing a side of ourselves that doesn't exist because we're trying to project a certain image to others. Perhaps you thought baking bread was a great idea and you had visions of serving your family homemade sourdough. Perhaps you bought all the ingredients, or perhaps you spent money on a bread machine. Perhaps you tried baking bread and hated it. Even if you don't like the process of baking, you hang on to the idea that it's something you love instead of letting it go to find what it is you're truly drawn to.

Most writers' fantasy selves include making a living

selling books. Writers with part-time or full-time jobs, or with partners who help pay the bills, introduce themselves as full-time writers even when the label isn't quite correct. I've heard many writers say, "I make a living writing," though later they admit that they work in a bookstore, work as freelance writers or editors, are content creators, or do something else to make money. It says something about the fantasy self of writers that they feel that the only way they deserve the label of writer is if they make their living writing.

Letting go of the idea that my life is somehow incomplete if I don't accomplish Great Things has been central to letting go of my fantasy self. I've spent most of my life working towards Great Things, some of which I've achieved and some of which I haven't. When I did accomplish a goal, there was always this odd silence in my head, a sort of existential crickets, since the accomplishment was never what I thought it was going to be. The reality was always far less grand than the fantasy I conjured. The desire to achieve Great Things had overtaken my life to the point where I felt like a failure if something didn't work out the way I wanted.

I decided I wanted to get my PhD while I was still in my Master's program. After 20 years, I finally took the plunge and entered a doctorate program. It took me four years to finish my degree (fast in doctoral terms). Two days after I walked across the graduation stage in my doctoral regalia, I realized that nothing had changed. My life was the same as it was before. I still went to the supermarket. I still cooked dinner. Not one person I passed on the street cared in the least what I had done, nor should they. I had wanted my PhD for 24 years by that point, and two days after I achieved it I realized that I was the same person I was before. It sounds obvious, I know, but it was a revelation to me. I remember telling a friend from my PhD cohort that in truth, the only place it matters if you have a PhD is on a university campus. Outside of a campus, no one cares. Really, no one. I had this burst of brilliance while taking out the trash. Here I was with this grand accomplishment, a PhD, and I was taking out the trash like I always do. I was still going through my days like always. Of course I was. What did I expect?

To go along with the PhD, I had a fantasy self of being a university professor, living a life of the mind, spending my days reading, researching, writing, and teaching my favorite subjects. I was able to work as a Graduate Assistant for three years of my doctoral work, making a grand total of $18000 a year. The experience was a Dorothy in Oz moment where she peeks behind the curtain and sees that the Wizard is just some dude. When I peeked behind the curtain of Academia, I saw that it was just some dude and not at all what I imagined.

Academia is a lot of begging for money in the form of grants and other funding, publishing pointless studies in journals that no one reads, or if they do read them it's because they're searching for citations for their own work. Not to mention the fact that professors in the U.S. are paid sad salaries. When I was nearing the end of my doctoral program and looking for faculty positions, I discovered that professors made $20,000 a year less than I was making teaching high school English. Yes, if you work your way up the academic ladder to associate and later to full professor, your salary will go up, but that's only if you're allowed a ride up the tenure track, and not everyone is. I had an interview for a full-time professor position at one of the most prestigious public universities in the United States and the salary was *less than half* of what I make teaching high school

English. I knew the salary going into the interview, but I thought, hey, let's see what it's about. As I was talking to the professors, my eye kept going to the email that stated the salary and I realized that I couldn't do it. Would my fantasy self have loved the bragging rights to say hey, look where I'm teaching? Of course. But wanting bragging rights was ego-driven, not reality-driven, which I realized during the interview. I mentioned the crap salary to the professors (not in those words, quite), which was the end of that job for me and also the end of my fantasy self as a university professor. I had to accept that my dream job didn't exist and I had to let it go. Letting go felt like an amputation, as if I cut off this piece of myself that I had held onto for so long. After I made the intellectual decision to leave the dream job aside, there was phantom pain. Am I giving up too soon? Did I not try hard enough? Despite my lingering questions, all the evidence pointed to the fact that I made the right decision. I was able to continue at my university as an adjunct professor, that crap salary supplemented by my full-time job, so I had a taste of university teaching.

When you're always chasing a fantasy self, you're never happy since you're always grasping after that, over there, whatever it is you think you need. When I have a bestselling novel, I'll be happy. When I have my PhD I'll be happy. When I'm a university professor I'll be happy. When I have this other thing, I'll be happy. The truth is, I've achieved a lot of what I set out to do. I've had bestselling novels, three to be exact, and I have a PhD. Did they make me happy? Yes, for a moment or two. But it's fleeting. The moment passes, and then I'm right back to who I was before, chasing after some new dream and feeling incomplete until I achieve it. It's okay to let go of a fantasy self that is weighing us down. It's okay to let go of dreams that didn't materialize for reasons we may never understand. It's okay to let go of goals that are unrealistic, unimportant, or unsuited to us.

What if I wrote without any particular end in mind? What if I write because I love to write, because I'm certain it's what I was put on earth to do? What if I wrote without any expectations and without any ideas of what the result should be? What if I existed without basing my happiness on any particular outcome or without concern about how I appeared to other people? What would happen, do you think?

7

ROMANTICIZE YOUR WRITING LIFE

Your problem is how you are going to spend this one and precious life you have been issued. Whether you're going to spend it trying to look good and creating the illusion that you have power over circumstances, or whether you are going to taste it, enjoy it and find out the truth about who you are.

—Anne Lamott

ROMANTICIZING your life became a popular concept during the darkest COVID days when we were in the midst of lockdowns. It may seem contradictory to talk about romanticizing your life after discussing the fantasy self, but the two ideas aren't the same. Living as a fantasy self means projecting a persona that isn't true to who you are. Romanticizing your life is about accepting your life as it is while having some imaginative fun along the way. Writers should marvel at life, and we should capture that sense of wonder in our words. To capture it, we should experience it for ourselves. How will we share our sense of curiosity with others? As Helen Keller said, "As my knowledge of things grew, I felt more and more the delight of the world I was in." Imagine Helen Keller's experience. As a deaf and blind person, she learned about the world slowly, understanding first water, and then everything else as it was introduced to her. How can we share our knowledge of the world with others?

Life on earth is an extraordinary gift that we've allowed to become mundane, which says more about our expectations than the wonder surrounding us. We see magnified lives on TV and in film and think our lives are boring because they aren't filled with a manic amount of drama. We create drama for ourselves by overreacting to situations that don't require such extreme levels of negativity. Dramas should be performed on stage or in front of a camera, not around the dining room table. Real life is about the commute to work, earning a living, household chores, family, and hobbies. Romanticizing your life simply means taking the time to notice what is good and making the most of it even when it isn't exciting.

I've heard that romanticizing your life can be a way to make yourself the main character of your life's story. As a *Downton Abbey* fan, on occasion I may allow myself to imagine that my afternoon tea is presented by Mr. Carson. Is it silly? Sure. But that flight of imaginative fancy allows me to find a certain joy in the moment I might not have felt otherwise. Writers have overactive imaginations—that's why we write, after all. We should give in to that imagination when the time is right. Do I enjoy my tea a little more if I imagine Carson has brought it? Of course I do.

I must have been living under a rock because I discovered the Dark Academia aesthetic only within the past year. I'm older than the general audience for such an aesthetic since I'm at the stage where I've been an adjunct professor instead of a student, but still, I love the ambiance. I live in an apartment, so I can't paint my walls or add wallpaper, but I added some small details to my desk to make it more academia-like. I have a small bust of David and LED candles (as I'm writing this, my cat Poppy is sitting on my desk, and I would rather not set her tail on fire with a real candle). I have old books on my bottom shelf and a pencil holder that looks like an old typewriter. I also have my white quill that I got from the Charles Dickens Museum in London. If I had to label my style, I'd say it's Light Academia since my walls are cream-colored and my desk is white. While I'm at my desk I feel like an academic. I am an academic, but I feel like one as I sit here. With more than 20 years of experience teaching students from kindergarten through university, a love of learning has always been at my core.

Is reading an exciting pastime? Not to watch from the outside. Seeing someone reading is boring, but what goes on in the mind of a reader is something the most action-packed film can't replicate. While I read, I'm living another life in another way in another time. Finding a good book is one of the easiest ways to romanticize your life as you find new characters to make friends with.

Sometimes, people romanticize the writing life in unhealthy ways. They take Hemingway's example too literally and think you need to be drunk to write. Or they think the old cliché about being a starving artist is true. Still, writers can gain a lot by romanticizing their lives. I don't mean presenting a false writer self where you pretend to be something you're not. Negative romanticism means giving into the perception of the tortured artist too broke to eat properly sitting alone in a shadowy loft drinking bottles of vodka. Positive romanticism means that I find joy in the parts of writing that would otherwise feel so mundane that I might stop writing altogether. Sitting here at my desk, listening to a Dark Academia playlist I found on YouTube and enjoying the moody piano music, drinking a cup of Earl Grey Creme tea I found at a loose-leaf tea shop two miles from my house—these are things that help me romanticize this moment as I write my dreaded first draft so that the process feels easier than it would have otherwise.

It's easy to focus on the negative parts of writing, but it's important to keep in touch with the sense of accomplishment that comes with putting one word after another. I love the challenge of pulling together my story puzzle where I have these disconnected pieces, and it's up to me to figure out how everything fits. I love to play with the shades and shadows of words the way a painter loves to play with shades and shadows of colors. Sitting here alone, wondering if I'm saying something to the best of my ability, guessing how to get from Point A to Point Z, propelling my way through a shitty first draft that needs endless revising—all of it can be frustrating to the point where I wonder why I continue to do this to myself. When I romanticize my stories, I slip into this other world as if I were living in it. That's when I know my writing is going well—I've left the real world behind for this creation of my imaginings. I take delight in my fantasy world when I'm able to frame my writing tasks in a way that makes them less burdensome and more fun.

I'm not talking about toxic positivity, the kind of magical thinking where we pretend that anything negative—emotional or otherwise—doesn't exist. Terrible things happen. That is the reality of human life on earth. We shouldn't strive to live in a place of light where there is no darkness. Such a place doesn't exist in the real world. Paul

McCartney said, "But with writers, there's nothing wrong with melancholy. It's an important color in writing." When our hearts are breaking, instead of hiding from the pain, we should allow ourselves to feel the darkest depths of our emotions. Sometimes, life feels too hard to see good anywhere. We do the best we can at any given moment. To paraphrase Maya Angelou, when we did, we did the best we knew how to do, and when we knew better, we did better.

Charles Baudelaire said, "Always be a poet, even in verse." Find poetry everywhere. It's there, even if you have to search for it. When I have a quiet moment, I allow myself to embrace whatever beauty I see directly before my eyes. My two cats sleeping on the blanket still hot from the dryer. The powder blue sky outside my window with puffing clouds. The upbeat crescendos of a Mozart symphony. Rather than wishing things were different from what they are, I accept them. And then I ring Carson for tea.

8

FINDING FLOW

No need to force yourself to do something the "right" way if it's not your right way. Your job is to honor your process.

—Andi Cumbo-Floyd

EVEN WHEN I'M so excited about what I'm writing that I can't wait to get back to my desk, as I am about the novel that is my current work in progress, there are times when I have to stretch a bit to find my creativity. Maybe I'm not entirely sure which direction the story is going. Maybe I don't understand a character well enough to bring them to life. Maybe I'm not sold on telling the story in first-person point of view. On days when the words aren't coming easily, I worry that I've used up every ounce of creativity I've been given. Then I remember what Maya Angelou said: "You can't use up creativity. The more you use, the more you have."

In addition to being a writer, I also have more than two decades of experience as a writing teacher. I've taught writing to students as young as five and as old as grandparents in their 70s. One thing I've noticed over the years is that writers need to discover their writing processes for themselves. It's tempting to want someone else—your creative writing instructor, friends in your writers' groups, or people you follow on social media—to tell you how to write. Many want-to-be writers want some kind of formula, a step-by-step guide for how to write their short story, their memoir, or their novel.

When I was a freelance editor, I helped writers fine-tune their manuscripts either for independent publishing or to query agents. One of the reasons I stopped editing was because I felt like the writers wanted me to tell them everything about their stories. They wanted me to tell them what direction the plot should go, what the characters should do, and what the characters should say—in other words, they wanted me to write their stories as an almost ghostwriter. Such writers came to me with first drafts with so many plot holes their stories resembled Swiss cheese. When I asked them about their vision for their work, invariably their response was, "What do you think?"

Writers should make decisions about their stories for themselves. Why write if you don't have a story burning a hole inside begging to be released? If you don't enjoy the process of writing, the process of discovering the plot from the inside out, and if you don't enjoy the process of unraveling your characters until you understand what makes them tick, then for heaven's sake, find another creative outlet. Don't waste precious time forcing yourself to do something you don't love. Maybe some people loved to write when they were younger, but now the process is no longer joyful. Maybe some people think they'll be perceived as more successful, more artistic, and more worthy if they can present themselves as published writers. Steven Pressfield said, "We must do our work for its own sake, not for fortune or attention or applause." If writing for its own sake doesn't appeal to you, then leave that fantasy self aside to make room for what you love. If writing is a means to an end, such as seeking public approval, then delve into those feelings and see why you need external approval for a wholly internal art form.

Writing and writing something people want to read are not the same things. It takes time to learn the craft of writing. Most of us are familiar with Malcolm Gladwell's 10000-hour rule, which says that it takes approximately 10000 hours of practice to become good at something. If you're not interested in engaging with those 10000 hours, with no external reward besides the elation that comes from following your heart, then find what makes you glad to be alive. In *The Creative Act*, Rick Rubin put it as well as I've ever seen: "What we create allows us to share glimpses of an inner landscape, one that is beyond our understanding. Art is our portal to an unseen world." We each have to find our own ways of creating and engaging with our unseen worlds.

When writers understand their craft, when they know the rules well enough to break them, that is when they find flow. That is when we can break through the Resistance that Steven Pressfield explains in his book *The War of Art*. Writers experience artistic flow when they are in the zone of deep immersion in the creative process. This is what I love most about being a writer. First, I make my way stubbornly through the first draft stage. Have I said how much I hate writing a first draft? Through the process of completing my shitty first draft, I begin to understand my characters, my story, and what I want to accomplish with that particular book. Then, instead of dillydallying, which I am particularly adept at when I'm writing a first draft, I realize that I can't wait to get back to that world. When I'm in the flow, hours slip by, the sun drops, the sky falls dark, and I don't notice. I'm not worried about this, that, or anything. My concentration is fine-tuned to my story; when I'm in the flow, I am not writing the story at all, but I'm there alongside my characters. I am not here, and my characters are not there. We are together experiencing the ups and downs of their complicated lives.

Being able to give myself completely to these imaginary friends is not something I learned to do overnight. It took years of practice, years of writing terrible books, and then years of writing less terrible books until I wrote something others wanted to read. Finding flow takes trial and error, sometimes decades worth of trying this and trying that and trying the other thing until we find what sticks. To make matters more complicated, what works for one project may not work for another, so we have to start the process again of finding the flow for that particular book.

Experiencing the gratification of being in the flow is an important part of embracing the writing life. Accepting the ups and downs and the pleasures with the pitfalls is all part of the challenge. Philip Roth said, "That's what you're looking for as a writer when you're working. You're looking for your own freedom." No one can give you that freedom. You have to find it for yourself. When you find it, you will discover your flow.

9

WHAT ARE YOU SUPPOSED TO DO?

Doubts may grow as shadows loom, when you're alone with your thoughts. Plant music, art, pics of the ones you love in the darkest corners. Harvest the fruits of your daydreams and rest. Water and sunlight to the best in you.

—Lin-Manuel Miranda

WHILE BEING a writer helps me to find the magic of ordinary days, a creative life can be a mixed blessing. As creatives, we hold stubbornly true to the leanings of our hearts. I love the "Big Magic" of being a creative person. I love that ideas come from nowhere and characters with complex, messy lives suddenly appear before me as if I were a conduit. Why these ideas chose me, I couldn't say. Austin Kleon said, "Ask anyone doing truly creative work, and they'll tell you the truth: they don't know where the good stuff comes from. They just show up and do their thing." When I do my thing, good things happen. My heart feels full, fascinating stories appear to me, and I have the privilege of breathing life into them.

Being creative also means I'm prone to doubt. It's easy to become caught up in visions of how we're *supposed to* be and what we're *supposed to* do. I've fallen victim to the dreaded *supposed tos* as much as anyone. I'm *supposed to* achieve this much and I'm *supposed to* make that much and I'm *supposed to* look a certain way. As a writer, I'm *supposed to* do x, y, and z or how dare I call myself a writer? It has taken years to accept that maybe some of those *supposed tos* don't fit me and never did.

It's hard work letting go of the *supposed tos*. I'm not there yet, and I'll never be there 100% of the time. However, I'm getting better at recognizing what feels authentic to me and what has been placed inside my psyche by living in my Western society. One way I've started letting go of *supposed tos* is through the way I view my hair. Crazy, right? But my hair signified my first major step toward living an authentic life.

I dyed my hair for the last time in May 2020. I used to love going to the hairdressers, and my hair has been every shade of brown, blond, and red. When I was in a more adventurous mood, I'd have the stylist add slips of purple, and while I was a PhD student my hair was magenta from roots to ends. At some point along the way, having my hair dyed became a chore. Instead of looking forward to it as time for myself, I began to dread it as the date for my appointment drew nearer. I was having my hair done every four weeks to hide my gray roots, which appeared after two weeks, but I refused to go to the hairdressers twice a month at $150 a pop.

My decision to let my hair go natural (read: gray) was lockdown-inspired since the hairdressers were closed, and when they opened again I didn't feel safe going back quite yet. I tried dyeing my hair at home and hated everything about it. I hated the rotten garbage stink of the dye, the mess, and the stained clothing and towels. Once, I stained my bathtub. Yes, you read that correctly. No matter how careful I was applying the dye (to my hair and not the bathtub), I always missed a spot somewhere obvious near the front of my head. Then I developed an allergy where after I dyed my hair I developed painful blotches on my scalp. While I was working at home, I didn't want to deal with the burning welts, so I let my gray roots grow longer than I normally would.

During this time, I discovered groups of women of all ages who had enough of traditional beauty standards so they let their natural gray hair show. Many of these women documented their transition from dyed hair to gray hair by taking photographs every month and sharing their progress. I didn't realize that natural gray hair was a movement, and that discovery triggered an "Aha!" moment. I saw women letting their natural hair show as a quiet act of defiance, and I'm all for giving it to the man. When dyeing my hair was fun, it was fine, but it was no longer fun. Why was I still doing it? I was inspired by these women. It takes courage to go against the norm, and the norm in my culture says that women should try to look as young as possible for as long as possible.

Who decided that men could go gray and women couldn't? Who says that gray is distinguished on men, but women look like their husbands' mothers if they let their gray show? Gray is just a color, and though we associate gray with age, there are younger women with naturally gray hair and they look fabulous. I started going gray at 19. I had been trapped on the hamster wheel of dyeing every four weeks because I believed that to show my real hair would be "letting myself go." No, I decided. Just no. I hopped off that particular hamster wheel, and since I let my hair do its thing I feel freer in ways I never imagined.

It took 27 months for the faded auburn dye to grow out. I decided to go cold turkey and let my hair grow out at its own pace since that was easier for me. I worked at home for a year and a half, which means that I was tucked safely away in my house through the worst of the regrowth. Trust me, growing your hair out naturally, especially if your hair is on the longer side, can get funky. My hair turned out to be a salt-and-pepper color; actually, I'm surprised it's still as dark as it is. I'm not saying that everyone should let their hair go natural. For me, letting go of my fear of exposed roots was an important lesson in self-acceptance. We all have our own lessons to learn. Each in our own time.

On the surface, gray hair and creativity may not seem to be connected. You can dye your hair and still be creative. For me, letting go of my perceptions of what my hair was *supposed to* look like falls in line with who I'm trying to become as an artist. As a writer, I don't want to be held back by *supposed tos*. I don't want someone else dictating how often I'm *supposed to* publish or what genres I'm *supposed to* write in or how I'm *supposed to* be on social media.

Writing is how I express myself in this crazy world. And if I can let go of the *supposed tos* for my hair, it becomes easier to let go of the *supposed tos* for my art. It's easier for me to write what is in my heart because I'm not held back by other people's perceptions. Paolo Coelho said, "Stress, anxiety, and depression are caused when we are living to please others." Choosing to be a creative person means that we take back the right to live according to our own terms. We demand the right to our self-expression even when it runs counter to how our society wants us to behave.

My culture values extroversion, but I am unabashedly

an introvert. My culture values partying and networking, but I'm happiest at home reading, writing, and thinking about reading and writing. My culture wants to dictate what kind of family I'll have, what materialistic products I need, and how many social media likes I should have. When you're confident that your choices are true, you don't mind what others think as much.

As I'm embracing the writing life, learning to let go of the *supposed tos*, as both a human being and a creative person, has turned out to be a very good thing. Frank Stella said, "I don't like to say I have given my life to art. I prefer to say art has given me my life." I couldn't have said it better myself.

10

FIGHTING RESISTANCE

Most of us have two lives. The life we live, and the unlived life within us. Between the two stands Resistance.

—Steven Pressfield

ALL WRITERS HIT a wall where we don't feel particularly creative. Steven Pressfield in *The War of Art* calls that hit-the-wall feeling Resistance. I've hit the wall of Resistance too many times to count, leaving me with bruised extremities and a soft-boiled ego. What happened? You name it and it was probably right. I was afraid of failing, or I was lazy, or I was tired of battling between what I wanted to write and what I thought I was supposed to write. There are those *supposed tos* again, always haunting writers. As Pressfield said in *Do the Work*, "We can never eliminate Resistance. It will never go away. But we can outsmart it, and we can enlist allies that are as powerful as it is." How do we fight Resistance?

A few years ago, when I was in a particularly bad bout with the Resistance monster, I found a few strategies that helped me through. The first thing I did was start a new journal. I can't say enough about the value of journaling for writers. It's so important to have space where we can write whatever we want, however we want, for our eyes alone. For this particular journal, I didn't write about anything special. I wrote about interesting things that happened during the day, things I was grateful for, things that annoyed me, things that brought me joy. Often, I wrote about writing. Why wasn't I writing? What was holding me back? As I worked through my answers to those questions, I could see a way forward that included writing.

Another time I hit the wall of Resistance, I was having trouble figuring out the direction my story wanted to go. Normally, stories come to me as if in a vision and I have little problem moving my characters from Point A to Point Z. For whatever reason, this story was stubborn about revealing itself. I put that project aside and began writing something else. In time, I was able to see how my characters moved through their lives, and in time I did complete the book that became *Down Salem Way*. In the end, I was pleased with the way the story worked out, but it was a struggle to get there.

I have also beaten down Resistance by starting Julia Cameron's 12-week course, *The Artist's Way*. It might seem odd that I should begin such a course at that stage of my writing life after publishing seven novels. I was doing all right, right? I was writing, publishing, and finding success where I could. I've always believed that you'll find what you need if you open yourself up to receive it. On a whim, I pulled *The Artist's Way* off my bookcase. The book had been sitting on my shelf for years, but for whatever reason I hadn't read it yet. I didn't need it before, and when I did need it, there it was waiting for me. I skimmed the pages and recognized it as a 12-week course that needed to be worked through rather than read cover to cover. In a moment of self-doubt about my creative abilities, I decided to take the plunge. Luckily for me, I had just reread *Writing Down the Bones* by Natalie Goldberg, and Goldberg's suggestions went perfectly with the purpose of *The Artist's Way*.

One of the tenets of Cameron's course is completing what she calls morning pages. If you're not familiar with morning pages, they are three hand-written pages of stream of consciousness, and they should be written first thing in the morning. I grabbed a clean notebook and wrote morning pages for the first time. I found them valuable since they took away the inherent fear that can come with putting untested words on a blank page—a fear that all writers, no matter how experienced, feel from time to time. The purpose of morning pages is to get the thoughts flowing. Natalie Goldberg refers to it as writing practice. I used Goldberg's idea of using sensory detail, memories, and life happenings as fuel for my morning pages. Here's a sample from my morning pages from that time, written while my mother was in the hospital recovering from surgery.

I have been to this hospital too many times to count. It is as though the hospital itself waves "Hello! Welcome back!" whenever it opens its sliding glass doors to me and I walk from the 115-degree dry desert heat into the cold, stale air of the waiting room. If I think about it, I can count the number of times I have been here: one...two...three...four...five...six...seven... My mother calls this hospital her home away from home, and it is. The hospital is located at the north end of Tenaya Way, the medical district with doctors' offices, physical therapists' offices, blood-draw offices, and MRI offices. There's also a post office and a pub for those in need of a pick-me-up from waiting in tight-fisted doctors' offices or hospital waiting rooms where people are packed tighter than pencils in a box. There is the serenity of the mountains in the distance, but there's also the freeway just a few feet away, and if you stop and listen you can hear the zoom of the car-chase speeds as vehicles zip past, as though the drivers believe they are race car champions.

I won't bore you with the rest of it, but you can see that I was writing whatever I thought at the moment.

Another tenet of Cameron's *The Artist's Way* is the artist's date, a practice I've come back to again and again. An artist's date, according to Cameron, is a weekly chance to get in touch with our inner creative. It's a chance to do something fun simply for the sake of doing something fun. I love to art journal, but it's something I tend to let slide for months at a time. When I was completing the steps of Cameron's course, I had great fun pulling out my paints and stencils again, and I was sorry I let it go for so long. With both morning pages and artist's dates, the only way to do them wrong is to not do them at all.

My Resistance is largely due to my inherent laziness. I have epic skills in procrastinating. Most writers do. I'm able to get the writing done because I know I'll be unhappy if I don't write. Steven Pressfield said, "Procrastination is the most common manifestation of Resistance because it's the easiest to rationalize. We don't tell ourselves, 'I'm never going to write my symphony.' Instead we say, 'I am going to write my symphony; I'm just going to start tomorrow.'" How many times have I said this? Or, more common for me is the old "I think I'll start on Monday..." Or the Monday after, or the Monday after. To overcome my natural sloth-like instinct, I rely on short assignments. I remind myself that it's just 500 words and it doesn't take me long to get those words written. The Resistance monster can be beaten down if you prove that you are stronger than it is.

11

DARE TO DO NOTHING

Stop the noise in your mind in order for the wondrous sounds of life to be heard. Then you can begin to live your life authentically and deeply.

—Thich Nhat Hanh

I DON'T ALWAYS NEED a months-long break from writing, which is good because otherwise I'd never get anything done. There are times when a day-long break will do. When I feel overwhelmed by the sheer number of things I want to get done, I take a day to do nothing. I don't plan anything for myself. I do only what I want, even if that means staring at the wall. I've had a lot on my plate lately, like so many of us. Teaching keeps me busy during the day, and there are days when I leave feeling physically and mentally drained, days when I'm not good for much of anything when I get home.

I don't know where the idea that writing is easy or glamorous comes from. I think readers see authors when they win awards or when they're nicely dressed on talk shows and think that writers have the life. Or they know about

Hemingway and think we drink all day. They don't see us when we're still in our pajamas at 3 pm or when we're shuffling along with bent backs like we're 100 years old because we've been sitting for hours. Writing can be exhilarating. It gives color to what might otherwise be a black-and-white existence. Writers love to talk about how wonderful writing is, and it is, but it can also be frustrating at times.

The mental focus that you need to tell stories can put a dampener on your energy, and there are times when the weight of my to-do list flattens me. If I'm going to lean into everything good about embracing the writing life, I must also acknowledge when things become too much. That doesn't make me less of an artist or a writer. It means I'm in tune with myself and what I need. When I take a day off because I need a mini-break, my instinct is to be upset because I'm wasting a day. There are times when I suffer from the "Do Something" syndrome. It's hard not to feel like I should constantly be working—whether it's writing, editing, marketing, whatever—or else I'm not trying hard enough.

Doing nothing is a hard concept for those of us who feel we have to go, go, go. On days when everything feels overwhelming, I've learned to give myself a break. It's not a good thing when we push ourselves so hard that we lose touch with our creativity. Thich Nhat Hanh said, "It's okay to make a wish, to have an aim. But we shouldn't allow it to become something that prevents us from living happily in the here and now." A day to sit back and watch your favorite TV show, spend time with family or friends, or simply sit near a window and watch the clouds glide across the sky can be exactly what we need to reboot. We need energy to face the next challenge.

Elizabeth Gilbert said, "I would like to spend the rest of

my days in a place so silent, and working at a pace so slow, that I would be able to hear myself living." Allowing ourselves time to breathe, to think, to simply exist can be the best present we can give our creativity. We need to infuse our writing with life, and we need to give ourselves time to live.

Authentic living is as important for writers as it is for anyone else. We need time to discover the ideas, thoughts, and dreams we will use as raw material for our imagined worlds. Daring to live more slowly, even daring to do nothing on occasion, can help us refill our creative wells until our cups overflow. How we fill our cups is up to each of us. I'm on no schedule on my do-nothing days. My only rule is that I'm not working or doing anything writing-related. I'm doing exactly what I want when I want, which is often what I need when I'm too run down to do anything else.

Rabbi Nachman of Breslov said, "May it be my custom to go outdoors each day among the trees and the grasses, among all growing things and there may I be alone and enter into prayer to talk with the one that I belong to. Know that every shepherd and shepherdess has a unique Negrin (melody) for each of the grasses and for each place they herd. For each and every grass has its own song and from these songs of the grasses the shepherds compose their songs." What a blessing it would be to compose our songs—our stories, our paintings, our sculptures—through deep communion with the natural world. What a blessing to connect to our authentic selves. We need to allow ourselves stillness to tap into that deeper part where creativity resides. The way to tap into our unique melodies is to leave behind the to-do lists, even for one day.

12

FINDING TIME TO WRITE

Write a page a day. Only 300 words and in a year you have written a novel.

—Stephen King

IT'S one thing to say we want to write 2500 words a day and another to find the time in which to commit those words to paper. I know I'm stating the obvious when I say that if you want to be a writer then you'll have to make time for writing. You'll have to dig into your determination to get 'er done because it's so easy to say, "Sorry, writing, no time for you today." To be a writer, you must write. Nora Roberts said, "A writer never finds the time to write. A writer makes it. If you don't have the drive, the discipline, and the desire, then you can have all the talent in the world and you aren't going to finish a book."

I said in *Painting the Past* that if you have a nice job, a nice family, and a nice life and you don't feel a compelling need to write, then you probably shouldn't write. Writing isn't for the meek at heart. It's for those of us who are compelled to do it or else we're a little less alive. Chuck Wendig said, "You write because you jolly well fucking want to. You write because you like it. Because it's a part of who you are."

Writing is such an integral part of who I am that I'm compelled to make life choices that allow me time for writing. I don't have children, which makes a difference in the amount of time I have to write. But parents write. My friend with twin toddlers writes while her children are napping and for an hour after they go to bed. Another writer I know has a full-time job and three kids. She writes during her lunch break five days a week and while her children are at music lessons or play dates. I know others who wake up earlier or go to bed later to write when the house is quiet.

It can be done, but you have to decide that writing is important enough to make it a priority. "Protect the time and space in which you write. Keep everybody away from it, even the people who are most important to you," said Zadie Smith. As creatives, we have to learn to say no, even to the people we love the most. But we don't have to say no all the time. Writers need to live so that we can infuse our humanity into our stories. To retain our humanity, we have to keep close to the humans we love. But we also need to protect our writing time.

Writers who want to publish many books a year will have to write at an enormous pace. I listened to a podcast where the writer said she publishes 12 books a year. She also said she works 18 hours a day seven days a week. That hectic pace must work for her lifestyle. I don't want to write 12 books a year, and I certainly don't want to work 18 hours a day.

It's easy enough to come up with excuses not to write. Trust me. I'm an expert at making excuses, which include pertinent conversations with my cats about the state of the world. Just a few moments ago I was skimming Feedly instead of writing this chapter. But I came back because I have things I've learned about writing that I want to share.

Finding time to write doesn't only mean deciding what your daily word count is going to be or how many books you're going to publish. It also means deciding how you're going to get those books written. Are you going to be a plotter, who works out the plot of your book before you begin writing? Are you going to be a pantster who flies by the seat of your pants and writes what occurs to you at the moment? I began my fiction writing life as a plotter, but over the years I've become more of a pantster, more of a discovery writer. My outlines are skeleton-bare, with just the vaguest ideas of what I think will happen. Notice that I said what I *think* will happen because new ideas make themselves known throughout the writing process. I also like to kick ideas around in my head for a while before committing anything to paper. This is my process. Your process will be your own.

We have to commit to writing even when it scares us. Steven Pressfield talks about the concept of the shadow career in his book *Turning Pro*. One of the examples Pressfield uses is, "Are you getting your PhD in Elizabethan Studies because you're afraid to write the tragedies and comedies that you know you have inside you?" Pressfield is referring to people who don't make time to pursue their passions. He points out the dichotomy between artists and addicts: an addict, in this case, meaning a self-sabotaging amateur who distracts herself away from her true passion. Or we play Gummy Drop for hours at a time (that last bit was from me, not Pressfield).

If you want to write, then you must find time to sit your bottom down and write. Perhaps you prefer to dictate your ideas into your phone as you walk the dog or do the dishes. How you get your ideas out of your head isn't important. What is important is that you commit to doing it whenever you can, however you can, for as long as you can. I've spoken to many people over the years who have burning desires to write yet they don't write. I have a friend who has wanted to write mystery novels for as long as I've known her, but she hasn't started yet. Whenever I think of people like my friend, I remember that quote from Maya Angelou: "There is no greater agony than bearing an untold story inside you." I wish I could help my friend realize that it's okay, you can do it, you don't need permission from anyone, do what you can do right now. It's okay if your work is terrible in the beginning. As Natalie Goldberg said, we must free ourselves to write the worst junk in the world. From the junk, we can create art if we're willing to try. Some people can be so afraid of trying something new and making mistakes that they talk themselves out of practicing until they become better. Yes, it can be hard to find time to write when you work full-time, but it can be done. I wrote ten novels, ran *The Copperfield Review*, and helped other writers edit their novels while working full-time as a teacher.

Being a full-time teacher doesn't stop me from writing. I'm revising this chapter at 3:44 pm on a Wednesday afternoon. I'm home from school, I've done whatever I had to do for tomorrow, and now I have time to write out these thoughts which you are now subjected to reading. As long as you make time for writing, you are a writer. Even if my friend starts by writing 500 words a day, 250 words a day, 100 words a day, whatever it is, those words will allow her to pursue her passion at a pace that's right for her.

There are also days when I don't get to the computer at

all. Do you know what happens if I don't write every day? Nothing. As in absolutely.

I had a cold two weeks ago, and I didn't write a thing for more than a week. There were no lightning strikes, no booming voices from the heavens. I gave myself the time I needed to get well, and then I started writing again. Embracing the writing life means that I allow myself to go with the flow instead of fighting against the current. The *musts* of being a writer can feel overwhelming, making me crazy, angry, frustrated, or all of the above. In *The Creative Act,* Rick Rubin says, "The weight of our expectations can grow heavy. As does the fear that we are not up to the task at hand. What if we can't pull it off this time? What helps to keep these worries at bay and move forward is trust in the process." I have been writing long enough to trust my process, and when I'm true to that process it never lets me down.

How can we find time to write? By making writing a priority in whatever way we can. If we have five hours a day to write, two hours, 30 minutes, our lunch break—whatever time we have, we dedicate it to writing. Van Gogh said, "Great things are done by a series of small things brought together." We have to make time for the small things to get to the greater things.

It can be helpful to decide how we're going to structure our writing time. We can look at examples from those we admire, but in the end, we have to decide what works for our circumstances. Even though I make time for writing around my teaching job, I love to see how some crazy-talented humans have crafted routines that allowed them to find the flow from which they created brilliant works of art.

My main man, Charles Dickens, had an invariable writing schedule. Dickens rose at the same time, ate at the same time, and wrote at the same time daily. Dickens' son said, "...no humdrum, monotonous, conventional task could ever have been discharged with more punctuality or with more business-like regularity than he gave to the work of his imagination and fancy." On an ordinary day, Dickens would write about 2000 words; however, during an imaginative flight of fancy, he might write 4000 words. Like any writer, he had slow days when he didn't write much at all. Still, he maintained his work schedule and sat at his desk even if he only stared out the window. In *Bird By Bird*, Anne Lamott talks about sticking to a daily schedule where we sit at our desks at the same time every day because it trains our brains to kick in creatively at that time.

Unlike Dickens, I don't always do the same thing at the same time. I've discovered that a no-routine works best for me. I write when I get around to writing, which is usually in the late afternoon after I get home from school. I've been writing long enough that I can usually access some creativity whenever I sit down to work. I do the usual checking of my email and the blogs I follow because what is the point of being a writer if not to procrastinate? When I run out of pointless things to do, I know I have to get started. Maya Angelou said, "When I'm writing, I write. And then it's as if the muse is convinced that I'm serious and says, 'Okay. Okay. I'll come.'" My muse is used to my odd hours, so she (usually) comes when called. I have an inherent recalcitrance, which means that I can't be told what to do. Someone will say to me, "Do this," and my response is generally, "Yeah, that's not gonna happen." I've tried scheduling my time by blocking out a work schedule on Google Calendar saying what time I should work on my new novel or what time I should edit a chapter of this book. My problem is that I create events on the calendar but then I never look at them since I don't actually care what the calendar says. I'll write when I write. So there, Google Calendar!

I've discovered that instead of scheduling my hours, I give myself one or two tasks per day. That's it. My two tasks today were to write this chapter and to complete the character outline for my new novel. When I get my tasks done, life is good. One or two tasks a day might not sound like much, but it's enough for me to make progress, and that's all I need—progress.

After I finish my task or two, I do a happy dance. It's a grandfather happy dance, but still, it's a happy dance. If you have a set time every day when you can write, and if a routine works for you, you do you. Scheduling tasks into neat little hour blocks doesn't work for me. It doesn't mean I'm not focused. It means I've worked through my ideas, I have a strong sense of what I want to accomplish that day, and I've decided which one or two tasks I'll complete. Calendars and planners work well for many writers. If they work for you, use them. For me, by not forcing myself into arbitrary boxes, I've discovered my own way of getting my writing done. Instead of feeling pulled in every direction, I know I'll be focused on the necessary tasks at hand. Over time, I learned to tune out any writing advice that declares I *must* do things their way. I learned to shut out noise from anyone who thinks they know more about my writing process than I do.

When will you write? Will you get up a little earlier or stay up a little later? Will you use your lunch hour? Will you put away the social media, the games, or the videos of other people living their lives? How many words will you write? If you're just getting started, a tiny goal like 100 words a day is fine. I promise, it's fine. If you learn about a writer who writes 15000 a day, well, bully for them. If 15000 words a day works for you, well, bully for you too. But part of making the writing life stick is finding a pace that works for you.

When I'm writing a first draft, I have a 500-word-a-day goal. It doesn't sound like much, and it makes me look like a right loser next to those who write 5000 words a day, but if I didn't have a small goal that I could easily accomplish then I would never write another word. If there's no first draft, then there's no second draft, and there's definitely no book. For my second draft, I don't count words as much as I work in chapters. When I'm at the editing stage, I'll edit a few chapters at a time, maybe two or three. The further along I am in the process, the more work I'm able to complete in a day because I have a clearer vision of what I'm trying to accomplish.

Embracing the writing life means that we get to experiment all the time. We can always try new things, and it's never too late to experiment with something different. "Writing is not like dancing or modeling," said Elizabeth Gilbert. "Your writing will only get better as you get older and wiser. If you write something beautiful and important, and the right person somehow discovers it, they will clear room for you on the bookshelves of the world—at any age. At least try."

Life is too short not to try. If you have a passion for writing, make time to pursue that passion. Natalie Goldberg said, "Too often we take notes on writing, we think about writing, but never do it. I want you to walk into the heart of the storm, written words dripping off hair, eyelids, hanging from hands." You're the only one who can write your story your way. Except the AI bots. Maybe the AI bots can write it for you. But not really. You have to take responsibility for finding time if you want to embrace the writing life.

13

WHEN I NEARLY GAVE UP WRITING FOR GOOD

The whole point of being alive is to evolve into the complete person you were intended to be.

—Oprah Winfrey

EBB AND FLOW is something we have to make peace with because it's part of the creator's life. Most of the time, we can balance the not-so-good times with the better times, and somehow we keep going. There are times, though, when the not-so-good can weigh us down, drown us, even. Between the years 2006 and 2009, I had finally gone under and I decided that I was giving up writing for good. That was my intention, at least—to never write anything other than a grocery list again.

I started writing seriously, as in writing books that I wanted to have published, while pursuing my undergraduate degree in English. My first novel, written when I was 19, was about a rock band. Yes, I know, but I was 19. The book was terrible, but it helped me realize that I wanted to be a writer. First, I was going to be a journalist, then a screenwriter, and finally, I realized that my talents were best suited to writing fiction. It took four years to have my first piece published, a short story in a small literary journal. Then, I wrote a historical novel. I had a couple of near misses with traditional publishers, but nothing panned out despite my high falutin' dreams. I wrote a second historical novel, and a third historical novel, still with no publishing deals to show for it. Mind, this was before the indie author revolution, and traditional publishing was my only hope for getting my beloved stories out into the world.

By 2006, I had written three novels, two screenplays, several short stories, and a few articles, to some success. I had a few articles and short stories published, but I was stuck. I didn't know what to write next. I didn't have another novel in me. First of all, I had no ideas, and second of all, I felt like it didn't matter since whatever I wrote no one was going to read it anyway. I had an idea to turn one of my short stories into a screenplay, but I wasn't motivated to get past page two.

During this time, I saw Jacqueline Woodson, the award-winning author of books for young adults such as *Brown Girl Dreaming*, *Hush*, *If You Come Softly*, and *Miracle's Boys*, when she came to speak at my university. Woodson talked about how she began her writing career, thinking that she wanted to be a great "literary" writer. Finally, she found her voice writing for children and young adults, and what a voice she found. She deserves every accolade that has come her way. I took Woodson's ideas to heart. Maybe I too needed to let go of any lofty "literary" ideals.

Despite Woodson's encouraging words, I still had nothing. At the time, I was working as a learning strategist at a middle school. I had my own office, and during my lunch break I would close my door and brainstorm ideas about what to write next. I jotted down scraps of screenplays, short stories, novels, and plays. Ideas galore. But nothing called to me, I had no motivation to write, and I still had this fatalistic feeling that whatever I wrote wouldn't matter anyway. Who needs this hassle, I wondered? I felt like I was punishing myself for a crime I didn't commit. I decided that I wasn't going to write anymore. I'm out. Hasta la vista, baby.

I didn't write anything for three years. Three *long* years. The main thing I remember about that time was that I was lost. I didn't know who I was. I felt untethered to the earth, detached from myself. I remember that I was angry a lot. Most of the time, I wasn't even sure what I was angry about. My heart told me in various ways, "Stop! You need to listen."

Occasionally, I had the vague thought that I should write something, anything. Always, I went back to the mantra, "Why bother?" I looked for ways out of my job because I wasn't happy. I thought of returning to a Hollywood job even though I disliked the work when I was there the first time. I thought of moving to California, to London, to New York, to the moon. Anywhere but here. You know that saying, wherever you go, there you are? Even if I had moved, it wouldn't have fixed what was wrong with me. I continued to flap about aimlessly.

In 2009, I was teaching middle school U.S. history. One day, standing near my classroom door between classes, I noticed nearly every girl carrying a black book with an apple on it. I asked one of my students about the book and she told me it was *Twilight*. A few weeks later, another student handed me the book to read. "I've reread this book too many times, Ms. Allard," she said. "I need to read something else."

I thanked the student and told her I would read it. Once I discovered that it was a vampire book I wasn't interested, but I was touched that the student wanted to share her favorite book with me. I figured I'd bring the book home and skim it a bit so if she quizzed me I'd know something. I didn't love the book, but I liked it well enough to read the whole thing. Reading *Twilight* prompted me to watch the vampire TV show *True Blood*, which prompted the question *what would happen to a vampire who lost the wife he loves while he lives forever?*

See where I'm going with this?

The last thing I was looking for was an idea for a novel, but there it was anyway. Ideas are funny that way. They appear when you least expect them. At first, I didn't realize it was an idea for a novel. It was an interesting question that occurred to me about a preternatural man that I kicked around in my head for a few months. One day, I remember it was April and we were off for Spring Break, I sat down at my computer and started writing out whatever I knew about this vampire and his beloved wife.

Getting back to Woodson's point about discovering her true voice as a writer for young adults, this was the same journey I had with the story then known as "The Vampire's Wife." Mainly, I was happy to be writing again.

Distance provides clarity. When I was trying out this writing project and that writing project, frustrated because nothing was sticking, I lost touch with the joy that is writing. I had to find wonder in the process again. As I was writing the book that became *Her Dear & Loving Husband*, I returned to writing with renewed energy and a hard-won appreciation for the role writing plays in my life. That's what my heart was trying to tell me. I couldn't stop writing because I am a writer.

14

I SHALL RISE AGAIN

In spite of everything, I shall rise again. I will take up my pencil, which I have forsaken in my great discouragement, and I will go on with my drawing.

—Vincent Van Gogh

Vincent Van Gogh was discouraged often in his life, but he continued creating until the end. I know from personal experience that discouragement in the form of rejection letters, slow book sales, or any of the other hundreds of ways creatives can be discouraged is disheartening, to say the least. Including the time I nearly gave up writing for good, I've taken several breaks from writing over the years. My last break was a year ago, and it lasted about four months.

During my most recent hiatus, I realized that I had hopped from one project to the next for 13 years. Beginning in 2009, when I began writing *Her Dear & Loving Husband*, through 2022, when *The Duchess of Idaho* was published, I wrote 11 novels, one nonfiction book, and a PhD dissertation, which is 200 pages and required more work than any novel I've written. At the time, I loved every minute of writing those projects. I had so many ideas for new books that jumping from project to project seemed to be the only way to get all of those ideas out of my head. When I began *The Copperfield Review* in 2000, I was lucky enough to interview the historical novelist John Jakes, and one thing he said that has stuck with me is how he hoped he would live long enough to write all the stories he wanted to tell. That's how I feel too. But after 13 years, with a pandemic and a worsening hearing loss thrown in, I was burned out, and I needed to step away for a while. For how long? At the time, I didn't know, but I'd been through burnout before and I trusted that I would know when it was time to write again.

After journaling about why I felt so exhausted, I realized that I felt as if my books were becoming the same ol' same ol'. I'm glad that the *Loving Husband Series* chose me to reveal itself to because writing those books has made my life so much richer. James and Sarah Wentworth have fans all over the world, and for that I will always be grateful. Fans love the *Loving Husband* novels so much that some of them have contacted me asking me to continue James and Sarah's story. For a few years after the final book in the trilogy was published, I said there's no more, the story is nicely wrapped up, that's all, folks. But then an idea for a prequel occurred to me, so I wrote it. Then an idea for a sequel occurred to me, so I wrote it. Then I wrote a novella trying the various stories together. I felt as if I should continue the series beyond those six books since that's what authors are *supposed to* do, right? If you have a successful series you keep writing in that series. I thought I would create a Diana Gabaldon-type career for myself, writing in the same world from different points of view for the rest of my life.

I had a few ideas for ways to continue the *Loving Husband* universe, but after writing *And Shadows Will Fall*, the novella, I couldn't bring myself to write about the Wentworths anymore. Realizing that I was done with James and Sarah was heartbreaking because I love those characters so much. It took a lot of soul-searching, but I finally came to terms with the fact that I wasn't feeling the pull to write about them anymore. I had to permit myself to let the *Loving Husband* books go. It was hard, but it was the right call. In time, a new story dawned on me in a new-to-me genre that got my creative juices flowing in a way they hadn't for years. Perhaps I'll write about James and Sarah again in the future. Perhaps not.

Letting go of historical fiction was another change I needed to make. I've been known primarily for historical fiction since most of my novels are historical. I was the executive editor of a literary journal of historical fiction, and I edited historical novels for other writers. But I've grown weary of the research required to write historical fiction, and my next two novels will be set in the present day. As with the *Loving Husband* series, I may go back to historical fiction one day, but for now, I'm looking forward to the challenge of creating engaging stories set now. By allowing myself to leave behind what no longer works, I created the space to write new stories that make me excited to sit down at the computer.

I've made other changes as well. I ran *The Copperfield Review* for 22 years before I had an inkling of closing it down. By 2022, I wasn't excited about running the journal anymore. Whenever we do something for a sustained period, we have to evaluate whether that something still serves us or if we're continuing out of habit. By 2023, I knew I was continuing *Copperfield* out of habit, and it was time to move on. *Copperfield* had been such an important part of my life. I was thrilled by *Copperfield's* reputation as a home for literary excellence, and I was honored that *Copperfield* became a respected journal that writers wanted to be published in. I loved that for 23 years, *The Copperfield Review* was the first published credit for many up-and-coming writers. But when the difficulties of keeping a literary journal afloat became too much, and the joy was gone, it was time to move on. I closed the journal in 2023. I knew I made the right decision when I felt relieved instead of upset. If something isn't working, we need to let it go, whatever it is. We need to be brave enough to make changes when they're needed.

I've often asked myself the question *who am I if I'm not writing*? It turns out I'm myself, with all of my unique talents and imperfections. We're important because we're here, and we're enough just as we are. I don't need to earn my place. I've earned it simply by showing up. E.E. Cummings said, "It takes courage to grow up and become who you really are." It also takes courage to look at your life, as a human and as a creator, and do the work your heart calls out for you to do.

During my most recent hiatus, I felt relief when I didn't have a writing project hanging over me. When the new story idea dawned, I went from feeling frustrated and limited in what I could write to great excitement at seeing what I could make of this new genre. I have my best ideas for new writing projects when I'm taking time off from the endless homework assignments. When I'm writing, my best ideas occur when I'm away from the act of writing, such as when I'm washing the dishes, grocery shopping, driving down the road, or reading a book. An English professor said that Agatha Christie had her greatest inspiration while taking a bath and eating green apples. I think it was green apples. It might have been sour plums. Whatever the catalyst, we must allow ourselves time to take those baths and eat those apples if we are to access our imaginations. Our best writing comes from our deepest wisdom, which we can discover only when we quiet down enough to hear our creative voices speaking to us.

Writing, I've discovered, is like eating—apples or otherwise. Everything in moderation. If you're discouraged, that's okay. It happens to us all. Figure out why you're discouraged, consider if perhaps you need to try something new, as in a new genre, or perhaps you need to let go of something that no longer works for you. And then you will rise again.

15

LIVING WITH THE SEASONS

Take time to enjoy the journey toward your goal while also being mindful that achieving your goal will not fulfill you completely.

—Meik Wiking

IT'S MORE difficult to feel the seasons pass where I live in Southern Nevada. We don't have much of a spring here, and autumn is all too fleeting. As I write this in late July, the sky is crisp blue, and the purple pointed flowers are blooming. I would love to be outside, but today it's 114 degrees Fahrenheit and humid from passing thunderstorms. I have a love/hate relationship with summer because summer is vacation time for me but I'm not a fan of the weather. When I have errands to run or a new coffee shop to visit, I go early in the morning and I'm home by 10 am. In cooler weather, I love to take walks. I love to go to the park. I love to sit on my little patio and look at the valley in the distance. Most people hibernate during the winter, but not being a desert rat, I hibernate in the summer instead.

Even though the weather may not be obliging here, I've loved living with the seasons since I was in middle school. My mother's friend Linda always decorated her house for the seasons. I remember Linda saying to my mother, "It makes the holidays more fun." My mother was inspired, and we began decorating when I was about 12. I continue the tradition to this day.

Autumn is my favorite season since the cooler weather is such a relief. I love the pumpkins that I get from the one pumpkin patch we have in Southern Nevada. I love that the trees in my neighborhood turn red, rust, and gold as soon as the weather turns. I look forward to seeing a tiny bit of New England splendor in October. And yes, I am very much a pumpkin spice person. Coffee, cakes, ice cream—you name it. If it's pumpkin spice, I'll try it.

Even though it's cold in the winter, I'm out and about. Cold is relative, I know. When I tell friends in New England how cold it is when it hits 50 degrees Fahrenheit, they laugh and say that's not cold. I have to explain that when it has been 117 degrees Fahrenheit during the summer, 50 degrees feels pretty cold. I have a friend from Alaska who told me that it drops below zero in the winter, so people run around in shorts and T-shirts in 40-degree weather.

I haven't always liked winter. It used to be my least favorite season. You've probably heard about hygge (pronounced hue-guh or hoo-gah—I've seen it both ways). I was curious about this happiness concept and I went directly to the source, *The Little Book of Hygge: Danish Secrets to Happy Living* by happiness researcher Miek Wiking. Sounds like a cool gig, researching happiness.

Wiking's book isn't groundbreaking in that it presents new ideas. The book's power comes from the way it simplifies an age-old concept—doing things that bring us comfort may make us happier. Hygge won't pay the bills. It won't eliminate illness or stress or traffic or deadlines. It won't help you past that shitty first draft of your new book. But by participating in activities that promote hygge, what Wiking describes as a feeling of comfort or well-being, we can, for that moment at least, find some much-needed joy in our lives.

The easiest way to understand hygge is to think of comfort. Reading a good book while sipping a hot cup of coffee, tea, or cocoa while we are covered by a soft blanket is hygge. Soft, fluffy socks are hygge. Sitting near the open window listening to the rain is hygge. Eating cake is hygge (yeah, man, hygge gets me!). Lighting candles is hygge. Walking in nature is hygge. Wiking talks about how hygge can bring people together in a positive way. You don't need to spend a lot of money, or any money, to experience hygge. Enjoying the sunset is hygge and doesn't cost a thing. Wiking's book reminds me that focusing on comforting things can have a healing effect.

Instead of having the fluorescent overhead light glaring in my face, I light candles and turn on my fake fireplace. I live in an apartment, so I have a plug-in fireplace. The flames are pretty and I don't have to worry about my living room burning down around me. I love coffee and tea, and hot drinks are high on the list of hygge-things. When it's colder, I love putting on my comfy jammies and fluffy socks and covering myself with a soft blanket while I read. And don't forget the cake! I appreciate that Wiking says it's okay to eat cake and pastries when the mood strikes. If you want cake, eat cake. Not the whole cake, but enough to satisfy the craving. We have to indulge ourselves now and again. Life is too short to live like toddlers in the time-out corner because we were naughty for wanting to indulge our sweet tooth. And it's too short to live like a baker version of the Soup Nazi from *Seinfeld*—"No cake for you!" Yes, cake for you. And cake for you too.

I was doing a lot of what Wiking talks about anyway—lighting candles, drinking hot drinks, and eating cake. But Wiking reminds me to do these things with consciousness; in other words, I need to be in the moment with what I'm doing and why I'm doing it. I'm wearing my fluffy socks because they bring me comfort. I'm writing because it brings me joy.

Writing can be hygge for me, especially when it's going well. On the other hand, preparing a manuscript for final edits, stressing over deadlines, settling on a publicity schedule—none of that is particularly comforting, but it must be done. I make a deliberate effort to make writing time more hygge-friendly. As I write this, I have Mozart playing on Pandora, my electric fireplace going (without the heater since it's hot outside), and my blinds are open so I can see the greenery and the hummingbirds poking their delicate beaks into the sugar water I leave for them. I rarely turn on the bright overhead lights and instead opt for a small desk lamp with a soft glow so there's no glare. Poppy, my eight-year-old dilute tortie, is relaxing on the recliner looking out the window for any passing birds, while Lillie, my two-year-old Siamese, is watching Poppy watch the birds. While I'm writing, I'm creating an environment that, while it isn't always stress-free, is still pleasant.

You may have noticed that the concepts of seeking magic in ordinary days, romanticizing your life, and hygge seem similar. That's because they are. No matter what terminology we choose, we can't embrace the writing life unless we find the joy that comes with everydayness. Making a common task special is a life skill most people don't have. It's a skill I'm still learning, but it's one I'm glad I'm cultivating. Seeing every moment as magical gives me the fortitude I need to sit here and write. And tomorrow I will write some more.

16

TAKING CARE OF OURSELVES FIRST

Keep good company, read good books, love good things, and cultivate soul and body as faithfully as you can.

—Louisa May Alcott

WE'VE all heard the flight attendants' maxim about how we must put our oxygen masks on first. If we're out of oxygen, we're unable to help others. It's the same with life in general. If we're overtaxed and burned out, then we're unable to be there for those around us. As writers, if we don't take care of ourselves physically and mentally, if our creative wells have run dry and we're run ragged from the myriad of things we have to do, then there's nowhere to go for the vitality we need to keep going.

Like other writers, I spend hours sitting at the computer. When I'm not writing, I'm reading, which isn't a physical activity either. We've all heard the experts: too much sitting isn't good for our physical health, and it's not great for our mental health either. I have to make a conscious effort to get enough exercise during the summer because it's too hot to go for a walk. Summer is when I pull out my exercise videos and I do yoga more often. Our bodies were made to move, not to sit all day. I know that eating healthy foods and exercising helps to alleviate stress and gives me more energy, but it seems that the more stressed I am, the more I sit and don't eat particularly well. Cookies, candies, and sweet drinks are more desirable when I'm stressed or under a time crunch.

When I was a young adult in the 1990s, thin was in, as in the beauty standard for women was being so slim that your inner thighs weren't supposed to touch. In retrospect, I wonder why I was so gullible, but it goes back to the power of advertising and peer pressure. When I lost weight, the reply was, "Wow! You look great!" Which leads me to the question of was I really so terrible before? We're social creatures, and we want to be accepted by the larger society. At least, that's what the commercials tell us. I was obsessed with the number on the scale and worried that I wasn't good enough if I thought the number was too high.

As the years have passed, I've become less concerned about what size clothes I wear and more concerned about how healthy I am. One nice thing about getting older is that, if we're lucky, a little more wisdom comes our way. Besides, without plastic surgery, injections, weight loss medication, and severe diets, who meets the standard of beauty perfection?

We've been hardwired to pursue perfection that doesn't exist, and the pursuit of that perfection only makes us unhappy and often more unhealthy. A few years ago, I watched Bill Nye the Science Guy's show on Netflix, and one of Bill's guests said that whatever size you are when you eat a mostly healthy diet and get a reasonable amount of exercise is the perfect size for you. I wanted to kiss that woman through the television screen. That's what we should be striving for—health, not perfection. We want to eat healthy most of the time but allow ourselves pizza or ice cream on occasion—not all day, not every day, but sometimes. I know there are health experts who claim that they never eat a bite of bread or a grain of white sugar, but I often wonder if such people are truthful—or human. It's always wise to cut back on sugar, but I'm not going to forget the joy of a chocolate cherry crumble from my favorite European bakery.

There have been times when I neglected my health. I sat at my computer all day, not exercising at all. I was neglecting yoga, exercise videos, and walking when the weather was nice. It became a vicious circle because I had no energy so I wouldn't exercise, but because I wasn't exercising I had no energy. I knew that my lack of physical activity was weighing me down, so I decided to get healthier. I have to plan a little to eat more healthfully. I have to shop for more fruits and vegetables, and I need drinks that aren't sugary.

The first thing I did was cut back on how much I eat out. I used to eat out several times a week, and it wasn't always the healthiest food. Now I cook in my slow cooker. Crock pot cooking is very much drop-and-go. I chop whatever vegetables I'm using, add whatever spices I need, and let the crock pot do its thing. A few hours later, I have a delicious, healthy meal with minimal effort. I don't mind eating left-overs, so I cook more than I need for one meal and I'll have leftovers for the next few days. As for drinks, coffee and tea are great since I don't add sugar. I've been adding lemon to my water to get me to drink more water, which I've never been great at.

I love fruits and vegetables, so eating more of them isn't hard for me. If I've been eating healthy and I decide I want a slice of that cinnamon raisin bread I baked, I'm not going to freak out about it. I'm going to eat the bread, enjoy it, and then eat healthy for the rest of the day. I'm focusing more on how I feel rather than pursuing perfection. The better I feel, the more creative I am. Because my body and mind are sharp, thoughts, feelings, and ideas are more easily accessible. When I sit too much or eat or drink too much sugar, I feel lethargic and simple tasks become difficult. That's not how I want to live. I want to enjoy my life, not feel tired all the time.

I also had to get out of my office chair. Once I'm focused on writing, and especially once I find my creative flow, I can work for hours. There's that tip about setting a timer (for 15 or 20 minutes), and whenever the timer goes off you should get up, move around, do a yoga stretch, or take a walk around the block. I haven't done this myself yet, but it's something I might try. I've been doing a better job of getting up and moving. I work for a while, get up and play with the cats. I work for a while, get up and make lunch. I work for a while, get up and pop in an exercise video or hit the treadmill. I've eyed those standing desks and I'm curious, but not enough to buy one—yet.

One of the most beneficial things I've started focusing on is remembering to breathe. It sounds ridiculous, I know, because breathing happens. One of my yoga teachers said that as we go about our days, we breathe too shallowly, taking in only enough oxygen to stop ourselves from suffocating. Breathing mindfully has worked wonders for me. One of the things I love most about yoga is the fact that the poses are meant to be done in conjunction with the breath. The first part of the pose is with the in-breath, and the second part is with the out-breath. It forces me to pay attention. I'm simply there, on my yoga mat, stretching out the tired muscles that didn't get much use while I was busy writing.

I also need to pay attention to the obsessive thoughts that take up rent-free space in my overactive brain. I've suffered from ruminating thoughts for as long as I can remember. If you've never suffered from such noise in your head, well done you. Ever since I was a child, I've created imaginary horrific scenarios of things that never happened and never will, and the thoughts are on a repeating loop, forcing me to see the scenes over again. I've never been officially diagnosed with OCD, but I wouldn't be surprised if I were one day. I check the garage five times before I drive away to make sure it's closed. I do several cat head counts (of two cats) before I leave the house to make sure the furries are okay. There are other ways I'm obsessive that I won't bore you with. Of everything I've tried over the years, including medication, the one thing that works for me is counting my in-breath and out-breath.

Meditation might seem a little woo-woo for some people, but it isn't really. All meditation means is watching your in-breath and your out-breath. For years, I thought I couldn't meditate because I couldn't stop the noisy thoughts from rattling inside my brain. Then I learned that the point of meditation isn't to stop thoughts from happening but to recognize that thoughts are simply that—thoughts—and I don't have to believe them because they're there. After these simple but profound realizations, I was able to settle into a meditation practice. I don't meditate for long—maybe ten minutes, some nights only five—but it's enough to help me steer my consciousness away from obsessive thinking. Making peace with my thoughts has been truly life-changing. "The moment we're able to really stop, both the movement, and the internal noise, we begin to find a healing silence," said Thich Nhat Hanh.

You don't need to pay for yoga or meditation classes, although if you prefer the community that comes from practicing with others, then do so. I prefer doing yoga on my own schedule. I usually practice yin yoga last thing at night because it helps to calm me down after a long day. There are wonderful yoga teachers on YouTube. Try out different classes until you find someone you like.

Rumi said, "The quieter we become, the more we can hear." In our increasingly noisy world, we have to make deliberate space for quiet. For five minutes. For ten minutes. For however long you can spare. I prefer to listen to ethereal music, which can be found on YouTube. Other times, when I'm having a hard time settling down, I'll set my meditation app for ten minutes, listen to the Om chant, and then there will be a chime letting me know when time is up. Some days, it's hard even getting to five minutes, but as meditation teachers will say, it's the sitting itself that's the practice, even more so on the days when the mind won't stop chattering nonsense. Watching my breath for five minutes, with no distractions, is a link back to myself.

I've always found it harder to create when my thoughts are waterlogged with worry. I become so focused on the excess that I can't find my way through whatever project I'm writing. Once I learned to make peace with my overactive brain, and once I learned how to settle myself into the present moment through breathwork, I've been able to tap into my creativity more easily. Normally, after I finish a book project, it takes months before I'm ready to tackle something new. This time, after finishing my last book in April, by May I was ready to go with a new story set in a new world in a new genre. I'm grateful for the creative energy I found as a result of taking the time to care for my mind and body.

Thich Nhat Hanh said, "The more space we make for stillness and silence, the more we have to give both to ourselves and others." Always put your oxygen mask on first. Take care of yourself first. It isn't selfish. It's necessary to have the strength to take on the challenges of a creative life.

17

A PLACE FOR MY STUFF

Contentment comes not so much from great wealth as from few wants.

—Epictetus

TOO OFTEN, following aesthetics or wanting our spaces or clothes to follow a certain style, we feel compelled to spend money we don't have. The truth is, you don't need tchotchkes to appreciate a creative life.

A few years ago, I read Marie Kondo's *The Life-Changing Magic of Tidying Up: The Japanese Art of Decluttering and Organizing*. While I'm not a minimalist by any stretch, I do think we tend to buy things we don't need. There's nothing wrong with buying something because we want it as long as we're in control of the decision and we're not going into debt for it. We live in a materialistic society and we're constantly bombarded with advertisements for this, that, and the other thing. After I read Kondo's book, I asked myself if I would be happier if I had more stuff. (Answer: no.)

I decided to make 2024 a No-Buy year for me. Since

January 2024, I've bought necessities such as food since I like to eat regularly, and I've replenished things like cosmetics and skin care as I've run out. I cut back on streaming and subscription services I no longer use, and I put the nix on buying clothing, shoes, and house decor. I have more clothing than I wear, my home is decorated in a way I love, and I don't need anything else.

Not only did I cut back on my spending, but I decided to weed through my belongings to see what I used and loved. I've donated bags of clothing I don't wear (some with the price tag still on them), CDs I no longer listen to, books I no longer read, and DVDs I no longer watch to a charity that resells gently used items. I even tackled my garage, which seemed insurmountable but in reality, took about three hours on a Saturday to organize.

I didn't get rid of stuff simply for the sake of getting rid of stuff. There's nothing inherently wrong with things if they are things you love or use. It's the stuff that hangs out in plastic bins in our garages or shoved into the back of our closets, things that we haven't looked at in years, that can weigh on our psyches. It has been years since I moved into my current home and looked through the things I had stashed away in plastic bins.

I know what you're thinking. You're thinking that the week I spent going through my belongings was time I wasn't writing. You would be correct. I didn't get much writing done while I was going through my belongings, but it was time well spent. I agree with Kondo that a cluttered home can hamper our best intentions to concentrate on work. When everywhere you look is over-busy with things you don't need and never use, it sucks up brain space—or at least it does for me, making writing that much more difficult since my eyes are drawn to the clutter. As I was going through my belongings, deciding what to donate and how to organize what I was keeping, I realized that this tidying up was necessary for my writing process because I was creating room to work.

Desks are such easy places to pile things—something about the flat surface, I think. If your desk is messy, it's often the clutter that captures your thoughts, not whatever it is you're trying to write. It's easy enough to get distracted these days by YouTube and Netflix without being distracted by our belongings. I love to color, but my old desk had nowhere for me to put my pencils and markers. The art supplies were scattered all over my desk, taking up every inch of space, and there was no room for me to work. I donated my old desk and bought myself a white desk (more of a table, really) along with a set of white shelves (both courtesy of IKEA) where I stack my coloring supplies. Now the rest of my desk is clear for my computer, and I have plenty of room to work. Having somewhere to sit and think without distractions makes a big difference.

I've always been a big believer in a place for everything and everything in its place. This is where organization becomes important because you have to decide where you're going to keep everything you need. All of my writing materials are located near my desk so I don't have to go searching for them. Instead of scrambling for paperclips, I know they're in the container in my top drawer. Little things make such a difference.

Many writers are now completely digital as a way to stop the avalanche that happens when we have handwritten notebooks hanging around the house. I've started keeping more of my work in electronic format. Younger writers are more digital than someone like me, who is old enough to have learned how to type on a typewriter. Yes, a typewriter.

You know, those old-timey things people use as decor representative of an ancient past? Even though I make use of the digital tools we have today, I'll always love the analog process of writing by hand. I still keep spiral notebooks for personal and project journals, and my book journal is handwritten. After reading *Journal of a Novel* by John Steinbeck, the journal he kept while writing *East of Eden*, I've decided to handwrite the first draft of my current work in progress. Steinbeck's process is fascinating to me. Steinbeck's editor presented him with a notebook, and Steinbeck wrote letters to his editor, along with other notes, on the left-hand side of the notebook and he wrote the first draft of *East of Eden* on the right-hand side. I haven't handwritten the first draft of a novel in about twenty years. In *Writing Down the Bones*, Natalie Goldberg talks about how writing longhand in spiral notebooks helps create a hand-to-heart connection with what you're writing. There have been studies that prove the point, but this is the digital age, after all, and I can type a lot faster than I can write by hand, so I understand the draw to keep our work digitally. Plus, if you don't have a lot of space, keeping notebooks can become cumbersome.

Marie Kondo talks about the importance of getting rid of papers since papers bring no joy. I had two bins and three cardboard boxes of old papers in my garage, and I finally shredded and recycled them. Some of the papers were so old I found a coupon from a clothing store that expired in 2009. No joke. If they're old papers, get rid of them. If they're papers you need, find a space for them and keep them together so you know where everything is.

To me and other like-minded souls, books are magical, sacred, and not easily parted with. Most of us became writers because we love to read. I believe we can only ingest so many words before we're compelled to spill some back out. But at a certain point, there just isn't any more room on our shelves. I'm not suggesting that we need to get rid of every book we own, but imagine how much nicer our space would be, and how much more meaningful, if we kept only the books that were important to us. I had more books than I had space to put them, and I never got around to reading some of the books I had for years. Like most book lovers, I buy books faster than I read them. Other books I read once and that was enough. I donated the extra books and kept only the ones I love and will revisit. I still have more books than I have space, but at least now when I look at my bookcase I see books that bring me joy. I have my shelf devoted to Dickens because in my world Dickens gets his own shelf. I have shelf space for my books because it makes me happy to see what I created. I have a few knickknacks and some photographs on my bookcase, and my coloring books are there. When I look at my bookshelf I smile because I like everything I see.

Mind you, I write this after arriving home from spending $60 at Barnes and Noble, so just to be clear—the book buying won't stop. As far as my no-buy year goes, yes, I have bought books, but I'm buying less than I normally would. I'm doing a better job of reading what I already have, and I'm more mindful about what I'm bringing home. I also have my handy-dandy Kindle, which allows me to buy or borrow books. One thing about digital books is that I don't have to remember to drop my book into my bag before I leave the house. I know many people still love having a book in their hands. I certainly do. If you bought a book and it sings to your soul, keep it. If you read it once and that was enough, pass it on to a family member, a friend, your local library, or another charity that accepts used books. Remember libraries? We can borrow books from the library so we don't have to spend money on everything we want to read.

Often, what we keep is motivated by how the thing makes us feel rather than the thing itself. The more honest we can be with ourselves, the more we can weed away anything that is no longer necessary. I want to declutter so I can feel more comfortable in my own home. I want to clear my writing space so I have room to flex my imagination. It's hard to settle your mind to a creative task when there are things around the house that need seeing to. The point of decluttering isn't to get rid of things you use or love. I'm not interested in living in a house devoid of personality with bare walls. I want my living space, as well as my writing space, to feel comfortable.

If you've never seen George Carlin's classic comedy bit about a house being simply a place for my stuff, give yourself a five-minute treat and watch. Carlin was always ahead of his time, and this bit is particularly funny in this age of decluttering. For me, at least, decluttering has helped me become more aware of what I'm keeping in this place for my stuff. Only now I need new excuses about why I'm not getting any writing done.

18

A SENSE OF WONDER

Instructions for living a life.
Pay attention.
Be astonished.
Tell about it.
—Mary Oliver

SOME CREATIVES THINK they have all the answers. They know everything about everything and they'll let you know that they know. If you pay them hundreds of dollars they'll even share their secrets with you. Do this for an international bestseller! Don't do that or your story will starve to death!

There are few absolutes when it comes to writing. Whenever I see one of those "Ten Ways You're Writing Wrong!" videos I either scroll away or watch if I want a laugh. Whatever rules other writers insist upon (Stephen King thinks adverbs are *bad*), there are always examples of well-known, well-respected authors doing that exact thing. Remember—everything in moderation. There is nothing wrong with adverbs. I agree that you want to use them sparingly (see what I did there?), but you will not die if you use adverbs for seasoning.

No matter how long you've been writing, it's important to remember that no one knows everything about writing because no one can. When you see a book about how to write a novel, what the author is really telling you is how *they* write a novel. There are as many ways to write a novel as there are novelists. It can be helpful to get ideas from other writers, especially if you're someone who is looking to write your first book. But the only way to learn how to write a book is to write a book.

Whenever I sit down to a new project, I have to learn how to write a novel all over again. Each project has new characters I need to understand, a new world I need to learn (unless the book is part of a series), and a new narrative tone. One of my favorite authors is Kazuo Ishiguro, and the reason I love his work is because each of his novels is completely different from anything that came before. *The Remains of the Day* is completely different from *Never Let Me Go* is completely different from *Klara and the Sun,* and so on. Ishiguro defies genre. While my stories aren't as varied as his, I also don't want to be tied down by expectations. When I was in historical fiction mode, I wrote novels about the Salem Witch Trials, a country house in Victorian England, a woman living in Biblical Jerusalem, and a woman fighting for women's suffrage in Washington, DC. The only thing these books have in common is that I wrote them.

There's always something new to learn when it comes to creativity. If you're a beginning writer, the best thing you can do is grant yourself the gifts of patience and resilience. Patience will allow you to type word after word as you learn how to become the writer you want to be. Resilience will see you through the times when things aren't happening as quickly as you want them to, or maybe things aren't happening at all. If you stick with it, and keep writing even when things aren't flowing, in time you'll finish your project and it will be ready for the world.

If you've been writing for a while but feel the joy slipping away, remember why you became a writer in the first place. Was it because you had a story to tell? Was it because you created a fantasy world and needed to share it with others? Was it because putting one word after another is a challenge that calls your name? Reach into your initial joy of writing. That will help re-spark your love. Beginning something new means not knowing. Not knowing how to form a cohesive plot or not knowing how to form a character arc. But we keep learning. We read books. We find writer friends and join writer groups. We take classes. We write, and we write, and we write until we have that "Aha!" moment and the pieces of the puzzle start to fit together. There is nothing glamorous about writing. It's a lot of sitting, a lot of thinking, a lot of staring out the window, a lot of daydreaming, a lot of staring at a blank screen, a lot of jotting ideas into notebooks, a lot of tea drinking. Why the tea drinking, I don't know, but I like tea so it's fine. In a moment of inspiration, the words pour out faster than our fingers can dance across the keyboard until, once again, we're staring out the window as more complete visions reveal themselves and our fingers dance once more. Neil Gaiman said, "This is how you do it: You sit down at the keyboard and you put one word after another until it's done. It's that easy and that hard."

Remember when you were a child and everything was a

miracle? I began my career in education as a kindergarten teacher, and it was one of the best experiences I've had in the classroom. I loved seeing the children laugh while their eyes lit up with wonder at the smallest thing. Everything was wondrous to them. The simplest activities—making bubbles from liquid soap and water and empty strawberry cartons and watching the sunlight reflect rainbow prisms as the bubbles floated in the white-cloud sky—made them giggle with glee. As we get older and life weighs us down, it can be hard to find joy in soap bubbles or sand castles, but it's important to retain that childhood sense of wonder. That sense of wonder is essential to the writing life.

Whether you're a new or seasoned writer, it's possible to connect to that sense of wonder. Be imaginative. Don't write by rote. Don't follow someone else's formula. Dip into that inventiveness that played pirates under homemade tents and created entire lives for the pirates. Be courageous. I'll bet that your favorite authors are courageous in the stories they tell and the way they tell them. Don't be swayed by the crowd. See the world with reverence. Dig deep down and discover what you truly want to write. Hint: whatever you love to read, that's what you should write. Don't begin by writing for publication. Don't begin by worrying about how much money you're going to make after your book is published. There are easier ways to make money than writing, and the money is never guaranteed. We should always begin creative endeavors from a place of love. If the money comes, it's a bonus. As someone who teaches creative writing classes for adults, I find that my students often want to know how to submit work for publication before their stories are even written. Anne Lamott said much the same in *Bird By Bird*.

Some writing gurus say that you should study your audience and see what they want to read, or you should see what's on the bestseller lists and see what's selling. That might work for people who are mainly interested in making money, but I'm not talking about writing to market. I'm not talking about writing for money. I'm talking about writing because you feel compelled to share the visions of your heart. Woo-woo again, I know, but I believe that creativity is an enchanted way of being in the world. Elizabeth Gilbert calls creativity "Big Magic," which is the best definition I've seen.

Writers should foster a childlike curiosity, and we should embrace that fascination with life. Go to a local park and swing on a swing. Take your dog and play catch. Color in coloring books. Finger paint. Instead of working on your novel, write a poem about a character. Write a letter to one of your characters, or even better, write a letter to someone important in your life and mail it to them. How often does anyone handwrite letters anymore? What a lovely thing to send and receive. Do as Julia Cameron suggests in *The Artist's Way* and take yourself on an artist's date. As Cameron said, the artist dates help to promote creativity because they fill our well with ideas, images, thoughts, and inspirations.

You don't have to spend money on an artist's date. Coloring in my coloring book or walking in the park admiring the Las Vegas Strip in the distance are great artist's dates for me. Though there isn't much of a fine arts scene in Las Vegas, sometimes something interesting will come through. I've always felt a special connection to Van Gogh, as so many others have. While I'm hardly comparing what I do to what he did, I feel a certain camaraderie with him because I also try to do something different with my art, something that hasn't been done before, at least not exactly in that way. When I write, I try to show things the way I see them rather than the way I think I'm *supposed to* see them. There's something about Van Gogh's use of colors, brush-strokes, and emotions that is truly unique. One glance at one of his paintings and you know it's a Van Gogh. A few years ago, I saw *The Van Gogh Experience* at Area 15 here in Vegas. The exhibit is in a large room with tables and chairs, and you sit down, order a drink (Diet Coke for me), and watch as Van Gogh's sketches and paintings swirl into life on the walls around you. The images morph from one scene to another, and the video display appears to be 3D in places. It was a pleasant way to spend an hour admiring the genius of Van Gogh.

Have I said how much I hate writing first drafts? I trick myself into writing the first draft by giving myself short assignments, and eventually, the blasted draft is finished. Then I put the story aside for what I call "baking time" so I can go back to the story with fresh eyes. After the baking time, the fun begins. I have a clearer idea of how to accomplish my goal since I've had a chance to think everything through. From the second draft through the final draft, I'm in Creative Heaven, shaping the story into the book I wanted to write in the first place. The underlying inspiration for all of my books began when I was a 16-year-old in high school: I wanted to write because I wanted to share my stories with others. When I hold onto that thought, I remember why I've dedicated my life to writing.

What prompted you to write? Was it a childhood love of books? Was it a favorite author you wanted to emulate? If you're new to writing, how will you dig down for the patience and resilience it takes to sustain writing for the long haul? If you're an experienced writer, how will you tap into beginner's mind to keep the spark of writing alive? Embracing the writing life is a choice. No one forces us to be writers. This is something we have chosen for ourselves. As with anything we intend to do for the long term, we have to find ways to keep writing fresh so that our love doesn't wither away.

19

BREAK OUT YOUR NOTEBOOKS

Fill your paper with the breathings of your heart.
—William Wordsworth

MANY WRITERS KEEP a journal in one form or another. If you're like me, you probably have several journals going at once. I don't write in each of my journals every day; I write in them as needed. I have a personal journal where I jot down observations about my life. I have a gratitude journal where I write down three things I'm grateful for each day. It takes less than five minutes to complete my daily gratitude journal, but when I look back over the things I've been grateful for (beautiful sunsets, a cup of coffee, a great book), it reminds me of everything I have instead of focusing on what I don't. I also have a writing project journal, specifically for my current work in progress. Recently, I've added one more journal to my repertoire: a creative book journal. I pulled out my scrapbooking supplies, watched a few videos on YouTube, and created a crafty journal where I keep track of the books I've read and write my thoughts about them. I've come to love the process, and I retain what I've read much better this way.

Some writers get caught up in how they keep their journals. It doesn't matter if you handwrite your journal or keep it as a digital file on your computer or your phone. You need to do what works for you. In *Writing Down the Bones*, Natalie Goldberg recommends getting notebooks with cartoon characters on the covers because it prevents you from taking yourself too seriously while you're writing, which is a great idea, especially when you're journaling, and nothing should be taken seriously.

One rule for your journal is that no one should see it but you. Hide it away if you need to, but your journal is your private space to explore and play. Keeping a writing project journal is one way to invite the muse to visit. It's the perfect place to brainstorm anything about your writing project. What can you write about in your writing project journal? Anything you want. You might journal about:

1 Ideas for characters (character sketches or character questionnaires)

2 Ideas for the plot

3 Ideas for setting

4 Ideas for dialogue: conversations between characters

5 You can work through scenes you're having trouble with

6 You can experiment with different points of view

7 You can talk to your characters and see what they have to say. They might surprise you.

You might even choose to write about topics outside your project to get your creative juices flowing. Sometimes, when I'm completely stumped about what to write, I start freewriting about whatever occurs to me. That opens my brain enough to begin to think about my current work in progress.

You can also use a bullet journal for your writing project journal. When I wrote *The Duchess of Idaho*, I used a bullet journal to organize my historical research about life on the Oregon Trail. Even a mood board can be a great way to gather ideas for a novel or any creative work. Writers focus on the written word, but you can use images in your journal as well. You could draw mind maps where you jot down all of the ideas that occur to you. When you're in the idea-gathering stage, there is no such thing as a good idea or a bad idea. They're just ideas. Write everything down. All of it, no matter how silly it seems in the moment. In my experience, it's often the craziest ideas that turn out to be the ones worth keeping. Writing for the sake of writing, getting the ideas out of your head and onto paper, is always worthwhile.

Creatives cannot work in a vacuum. Your journal is a place to put your ideas together so that whenever you're stumped or you need some inspiration, you have easy access to your sparks of inspiration. The whole purpose of this type of journaling is to create a nonjudgmental zone where we feel free to play. It's only through writing the not-so-good words that we can find the better words.

Journaling teaches us that it's okay to create just for the sake of creating. It's okay to write out our thoughts, feelings, and ideas for the sole purpose of thinking on paper. If you're keeping a book project journal as I do, most of the ideas you try in your journal won't end up in your finished product. That's okay. Your mind had to work its way through all the possibilities before settling on the one that works. However you choose to keep a journal, you'll find the time well spent. It's important to exercise the creative part of our brains so that we can learn to become comfortable with the process of letting our ideas flow.

If you're looking for a specific way to use one of the many empty notebooks writers tend to have lying around, you might try keeping a commonplace book. I started keeping a commonplace book last year after seeing many posts about commonplacing. Once I discovered what commonplace books were, I was surprised I hadn't kept one before. Then I realized that I had kept commonplace books, only I called them quote journals.

The simplest way to understand a commonplace book is to consider it a receptacle of knowledge. A commonplace book is a place to keep your favorite quotes and passages from books, memes, movies, TV shows, and research. Perhaps you read something important you would like to remember. Perhaps you see quotes you would like to keep. You could write those important pieces of wisdom into your commonplace book. A commonplace book is a place to record any new knowledge you'd like to remember. John Locke said, "Reading furnishes the mind only with materials of knowledge; it is thinking that makes what we read ours."

Commonplace books have been kept for centuries. Commonplace books so inspired John Locke he wrote a book about them. Some noteworthy people who kept commonplace books are Leonardo da Vinci, Thomas Jefferson, Samuel Taylor Coleridge, Mark Twain, and Virginia Woolf, among many others. Such notebooks are intended to be a place to explore ideas and keep information. Leonardo da Vinci's commonplace book is a thing of wonder. I have a commonplace book with all of the wisdom I've found about embracing the writing life. Some of the quotes I have in my commonplace journal made it into the book you are now reading. I have quotes from writers, spiritual teachers, artists, creatives, Brené Brown, Julia Cameron, and Tasha Tudor; really, a wide variety of sources. As I'm working on these chapters, I have my handy-dandy apple-green commonplace book at my side, and when I'm looking for a quote from Anne Lamott, for example, I know where to find it since I added an index with page numbers so I can find the specific quote I need. I keep track of the quote, the author, and the book or website where I found it in case I need to access the original source again. You don't need to use a commonplace book specifically for a project as I have. You can keep a notebook with inspirational quotes that will get you going when your creative juices are running low. You can use it to doodle and work through ideas. You can add images as Leonardo Da Vinci did.

Commonplace books can be used to boost our creativity. Since there aren't many brand-new ideas waiting to be discovered, creativity happens when we look at what others have done before us, reframe it, and make it our own. Creating a commonplace book gives us space where we can take information from others, study it, synthesize it, form our own ideas, and learn from it. Afterward, we'll have a deeper understanding that will allow us to create something uniquely our own. That's so true in writing, isn't it? There aren't any new stories to be told. We're all simply retelling the same tales in our own ways. We study our influences, learn from them, and from that new knowledge we can create a style all our own. Then, we tell the stories the way only we can.

20

JOYS OF ART JOURNALING

Unused creativity is not benign. It metastasizes. It turns into grief, rage, judgment, sorrow, shame.
—Brené Brown

As CREATIVE PEOPLE, we should learn to embrace our imagination in all of its forms. I love writing, but I also enjoy being artistic in other ways. Time away from my writing desk helps to fill my creative well. There are various ways of journaling, and all of them are important to the artist's soul. I thought I'd share a bit about art journaling since I've found it to be another way to tap into my imagination. Perhaps this chapter will allow you to think about different ways you might be creative. All creativity is good for the writer's soul.

I learned to love art as an undergraduate student when I took an art history class. I didn't know much about art then, but the class fulfilled a liberal arts requirement, so I grabbed it. The class covered the earliest cave paintings in France through the Roman Empire. I remember how the professor seemed ancient to my 19-year-old eyes but was probably in his mid-forties, not old to me now, of course. He was a slight, slender man in khaki pants, polo shirts, and sweaters tied around his neck, though it was summer in the San Fernando Valley in California and 100 degrees Fahrenheit. I don't think I've ever seen anyone as excited about their subject as that professor was. He spoke with such enthusiasm, describing the hieroglyphics inside the Egyptian pyramids as though they were indeed handed down by the gods. One day, the professor led a class expedition to the old J. Paul Getty Museum in Malibu, and I was enchanted as I studied the Greek statues and pottery. I found the professor, and his subject, endearing, and it was because of that class that I developed a lifelong love for art.

As much as I love to visit museum exhibitions, I never thought of myself as an artist. I'm a writer, so I contented myself with creative expression in the form of words on paper. I dabbled in acrylic painting, but that didn't last long. I tried to take a painting class at the extension university where I was teaching creative writing, but the teacher wasn't all I hoped she would be. She was a short French woman with the oddly elfin look of Dobby from the Harry Potter books. Her dyed jet-black hair was cut into an ear-length 1920s flapper's bob, and she wore round black glasses that took up the whole of her face. She tottered around the classroom shrugging at the students' paintings the way only the French can. There was no instruction. There were no directions. She put some flowers in a vase on a stool at the front of the classroom and told us to paint what we saw. I looked around the classroom and saw students painting, but I didn't know where to start. I had never taken an art class.

Yes, I love to look at paintings, but looking and painting are two different things. I started painting the flowers in the vase the best I could.

Dobby stopped beside me and shrugged. "You are supposed to paint what you see," she said. "This is what you see?" Before I could answer, she shrugged and moved on. A while later, she stopped near me again.

"Why is your canvas so small?" she asked. It was my turn to shrug (I'm French too). I didn't remember there being a canvas size requirement in the class materials list, I said. Dobby opened her arms wide. "If you want to learn to paint, you paint big!"

I told her I didn't think I was going to learn how to paint from her if she didn't give any instructions. I was a complete beginner and knew nothing about painting. Her only response was "Hmpf!" as she tottered away. Another student next to me said that was just the way the teacher was. I grabbed my materials, left the room, and got a refund for the money I paid for the class. I practiced a little on my own, but I didn't know what I was doing so I stopped. I still considered myself a wanna-be artist, but I limited my non-writing artistic experiences to watching craft shows on TV.

One Saturday afternoon I was watching one of my favorite craft shows, *Scrapbook Soup* with Julie Fei-Fan Balzer, and she had a guest who talked about art journaling. Certainly, I knew what journaling was. Like most writers, I've been keeping a written journal for most of my life, but art journaling was something new. If you're not familiar with art journaling, it's the same as written journaling, except you're using art supplies like colored pencils, paints, stencils, and stamps. Just as with written journaling, art journaling is about the process and not about the finished product.

When we keep writing journals we don't worry about what we're writing—we're just writing. Art journaling is art practice. We're playing with the supplies, trying out different paints, different styles, and different color combinations without worrying about the final result. You can art journal on whatever paper you have handy—a bound journal, a composition book, even junk mail, old books, or magazines. You don't need to take art classes. It's the same learning-by-doing mentality that helped me become a writer, and since no one is going to see my art journal but me, I don't have to worry about some Dobby hovering over my shoulder shrugging as if I had no business so much as passing an art supply store.

When I began art journaling, I started slowly, buying some cheap acrylic paint at the discount store, and I already had a stash of colored pencils, crayons, and markers. I had an old sketchbook from the Dobby days and that became my art journal. I love stencils because I don't have to worry about my drawing skills. I had a box of patterned scrapbook paper since I've created scrapbooks on occasion. Art journaling is about expressing yourself however you want to in that moment.

If you're anything like me and have suffered from compare-itis, you'll find that it's easy to fall into that trap when art journaling. People who make art journaling videos or post their artwork on social media are professional artists, so it's easy to look at their examples and think, "Well, I suck. What's the point?" But that goes against the purpose of art journaling. You need to look at the examples as what they are—examples—and then do what you can at that moment. You can make your art journal pages look like scrapbook pages, calendar pages, or bullet journals. You can paint flowers, stencil flowers, or doodle flowers. If you try something and don't like it, you can paint over it with gesso or work with it. The only way to do it wrong is to not do it at all. Art journaling was invented for someone like me who loves to play with paint and color. Some of my pages are kind of cool, some are kind of weird, and some are kind of cartoony, but it's all good. Anything I do in my art journal is right for me. So there, Dobby!

If you're wondering how to use art journaling to help your writing, you can use it to work through ideas for your book projects. You could storyboard scenes from your story in your art journal. You could draw or paint portraits of your characters or the setting. You could piece together a collage of various scenes from your story. I drew a map of the university campus where my current work in progress takes place to help me visualize where one building is in relation to another. The only limit is the limit of your imagination.

Don't worry about how "good" your art is. This journal is for your eyes only, and it's not something you're going to hang on a museum wall. Draw stick people. I do. Your art journal is a no-judgment zone where you're playing with images and ideas. I studied mixed media journaling as part of my PhD dissertation, so I'm biased about the benefits of such a practice. I won't bore you with the details, but there's research about how the mixed-media approach helps people think more deeply.

Art journaling is a great way to unleash the inner creative. Anything that sparks our inspiration, whether it's a written journal, an art journal, reading books by other authors, baking new recipes, or going for a walk, will become important for our writing. It all goes into the well.

Spending time with my art journal reminds me that I'm a creative person. As a writer, I need to keep my creativity close. If you're interested in trying art journaling, you can grab any old notebook, buy some inexpensive paints, colored pencils, or crayons, maybe a few stencils, and get started. You don't need a ton of supplies. You can art journal on junk mail or whatever paper you have around the house. Being creative means many things, but mainly it means having fun.

21

COLOR ME CREATIVE

How much of our lives is frittered away—spoiled, spent, or sullied—by our neurotic insistence on perfection?

—Sarah Ben Breathnach

Even before I began art journaling, I started to color in coloring books again. Coloring is stress-free for me since someone else has created the drawing. All I have to do is choose which colors I'm going to use and fill in the blanks. I loved coloring when I was a kid, and I still love it. While coloring in a coloring book isn't creating an original work of art, it allows me to express myself in a way that's different than writing.

There is a meditative quality to coloring since the act itself is all I'm thinking about while choosing which picture to fill in, which supplies I'll use (crayons, colored pencils, or gel pens), and which color palette. The more I have on my to-do list, and the more stressed I feel, the more I appreciate the simplicity of sitting down with some crayons and coloring in some pictures.

A few years ago, when coloring for adults exploded in popularity, there were countless articles about *the right way* to color. The explosion of experts was similar to what happened with independent publishing about a decade ago—suddenly everyone was an expert shouting about the right way to write, the right way to publish, and the right way to market. The same thing happened to coloring. Something that should be relaxing became stressful as I tried to keep up with the *right* way to do things. There's nothing like an expert to take the fun out of something. I had the realization (while coloring, of course) that my attitude toward coloring was the same as my attitude toward writing. I had to decide for myself how I wanted to color, just like I had to decide for myself how I wanted to write.

First of all, use the colors you want to use.

The coloring experts will tell you to choose your palette first—use a color wheel to help you determine which colors to use. They'll tell you which colors go with each other, and if you use that other color combination, look out! The Crayola Police will hunt you down. That's how professionals do it, they say, so that's how you should do it too.

In time, I understood that I could use any color combination I wanted, just as I could write my stories however I wanted. I don't like choosing my colors ahead of time. I like to choose my colors one by one as I'm filling in the picture. Sometimes I have an overall idea of the color scheme I want to use, sometimes I don't. Sometimes I'm happy with how the pictures turn out, sometimes I'm not. When I'm writing, I have an overall idea of how I want the story to turn out, but I've also learned to get out of my own way and allow the story to find its path. If I prefer choosing my colors as I go as opposed to choosing them first then I can do that. If I prefer letting my stories find their own way, I can do that too.

Then, stop comparing yourself to others.

Just as with art journaling, there are some amazing coloring sites where professional artists post their finished pages. Some of those colored pages are indeed museum-ready. They're beautiful, with shading, light, and blended colors. I'm not a professional artist, so my pictures don't look like that. I love playing with colors, and some color combinations I like, some not as much, but so what? I wouldn't know what I liked unless I allowed myself the freedom to experiment. I have no desire to become a professional artist. When I have time to play with my crayons or colored pencils, I don't want to spend that time stressed because my picture doesn't look like that of a professional artist.

It comes back to compare-itis. Writers are always looking to see which writers are selling more books, getting better reviews, or winning more awards. We have to remind ourselves that we're not in competition with other writers. This isn't a race. Our lives as creatives are just as unique as our lives as people. No two are alike, and we need to focus on ourselves. Like runners, if we keep looking back to see who is behind us, we'll lose steam. We want to keep the momentum going forward.

Finally, outline if you want to, and it's okay to color outside the lines.

When I was reading posts with coloring tips, some experts said not to outline your drawing. Apparently, with outlining you're not going to have a realistic result and that's not how the professionals do it. I've always liked to outline my coloring pages. Even when I was a kid, I'd outline the shapes with crayons. Sometimes I'll outline with a darker color and fill in the shape with a lighter color. Is it wrong?

Not to me. It's my coloring page, and I'm going to do it the way I want to. It's the same with coloring outside the lines. I like it when my coloring pencils or crayons end up outside the line because then when I'm filling in the next color they blend a bit. How annoying, to feel like your coloring page is all wrong if your hand slipped and some color ended up on the other side of the line.

Once I went out to dinner with a friend who was about to retire from her teaching career. I told her about coloring and how many hours of enjoyment it brought me. I bought her some colored pencils and coloring books as a retirement present. A few months later, I asked her how she liked her coloring books. She told me that she was afraid to try them because she could never stop herself from coloring outside the lines. I tried to explain that this was her book for her enjoyment. No one was going to grade her, and if she wanted to draw big, squiggly spirals outside the lines, who was going to know? I don't think she ever tried coloring because she was afraid of some giant imaginary finger in her brain shaking "NO!" if her pencil strayed over the line. So often, the limitations we set upon ourselves are far harsher than anything the outside world could put on us.

Here are my tips for coloring and writing.

1. Color the picture that sings to you. You don't have to start at the beginning of the book. You decide where to start. If you don't love the picture, coloring it will be a chore, and you'll never finish it. The same goes for writing. Write something you're excited to get back to. If you're not excited about it, it's going to be hard to convince readers that your writing is worth their time.

2. Choose your own colors. You can choose your color scheme ahead of time, or you can choose it at the moment, whichever feels right to you. For writing, you get to decide

how you use language. You have the final say in how you'll string phrases together. You may not like the way some of it turns out. That's okay. You tried it, you didn't like it, so try again until you find something you do like.

3. Don't compare your pictures (or your writing) to anyone else's. Find your own style. That's how you'll find true enjoyment as a creative person.

4. Coloring (and writing) should be fun. Listen to your favorite music. Turn off your electronic devices and other distractions. Make your coloring (and your writing) time special so you're looking forward to getting back to it.

You can let the experts tell you what to do and how to do it, or you can find your own way. Whether I'm coloring or writing, I find it a lot more fulfilling to find my way.

22

ACCEPTING REJECTION

You must keep sending work out; you must never let a manuscript do nothing but eat its head off in a drawer. You send that work out again and again, while you're working on another one. If you have talent, you will receive some measure of success—but only if you persist.

—Isaac Asimov

When we commit ourselves to embracing the writing life, we bare our souls on paper for all the world to see. Even if we write fiction and tell stories about imaginary friends, we know that there are big pieces of ourselves in there. Maybe it's not obvious to the casual observer, but we know. We feel our nakedness in front of prying eyes. For a writer, nothing is more difficult than taking months, even years, to bring a project to life, sharing it with others, and then having that work rejected in one way or another.

Unfortunately, there isn't much we can do about rejection. Rejection is part of the creative life. If our work isn't right for a certain agent or editor, then it isn't right. Rejection is like anything else—the only thing we can control is our reaction to it. It can help to think of rejection letters as a way of learning where your work doesn't belong. A rejection letter is simply a sign that you need to keep searching for the right home. It also helps to remember that rejection letters aren't necessarily about the quality of your work. Editors have many reasons for turning down a piece. It happened all the time at *The Copperfield Review*. There were times when I turned down a piece I thought was well-written but it wasn't right for the journal at that time.

Writers think that "this isn't right for us at this time" is a throwaway phrase in an editor's attempt to be polite, but there is truth in the sentiment. Sometimes a piece was too similar to something I had just published. Sometimes a piece wasn't quite ready for publication (maybe it needed more editing or more fine-tuning). Sometimes an author had just been published in our journal and I wanted to make space for new authors. Sometimes the author didn't follow the submission guidelines and submitted stories that were longer than the stated word length, or the story wasn't historical fiction. There are many reasons why your piece might be turned down by journals.

As a writer, I hated the form letter rejections. I felt like the editors should tell me why they didn't publish my work. After I became an editor, I understood why form letters are a necessary evil. At *Copperfield*, I received hundreds of submissions per quarterly edition. The editorial team was me. Sometimes one other person and me, but really, I was it. Reviewing submissions, rereading them, reading them again, deciding which to publish, formatting the journal, contacting the authors—honestly, I can't even guess how many hours I spent working on *Copperfield* over 20 years—and I did it while working a full-time job and writing my own books. There is no way I could have written personalized letters to each author. I know it feels like a slight to writers not to get feedback, but it's important to remember that editors are people and only have so many hours in the day.

Beyond the amount of time such individualized letters would take, it's important to remember that the opinions you would receive are simply one editor's point of view. Just because I thought the pacing was too slow, there was no character development, or the dialogue was too stiff doesn't mean that another editor would think the same. It happened many times when pieces were rejected by other editors, but I published them. Other times I passed on something, but another editor loved it. This is why it's so important to learn to trust our unique artistic voices. Saul Bellow said, "I discovered that rejections are not altogether a bad thing. They teach a writer to rely on his own judgment and to say in his heart of hearts, 'To hell with you.'" When you believe in yourself, your author's voice, and your unique vision, then rejections aren't such a severe blow to your self-esteem. Stop looking to everyone else to tell you whether your stories are good or bad. Learn to be your own best judge about whether your story works or not. Writers need to trust their visions for their creative work. That doesn't mean that we ignore all suggestions, but it does mean that we learn how to judge which suggestions will improve our work and which won't.

I'm speaking from the point of view of a former editor of a literary journal, but the same logic applies to literary agents and book publishers. Rejections from literary agents don't necessarily mean that your book isn't good. Sometimes it might mean that your book needs more polishing, but it might also mean that they already have enough clients in the genre that you write in, or it might mean that the genre you write in isn't selling at the moment.

In 2010, *Her Dear & Loving Husband* was finished and ready for its close-up. I began the usual rounds of querying agents, hoping for representation as I had with previous projects. I wasn't thrilled at the prospect of going through the self-immolating act of querying agents again, and in 2010, independent publishing was just getting off the ground. Of the ten agents I queried, seven asked for full manuscripts. Ultimately, they all passed. Six of the seven agents said the same thing: I love the story, and I see your talent, but I don't know who to sell this to. What was I supposed to do with comments like that?

The problem, I discovered, is that *Her Dear & Loving Husband* doesn't fall neatly into a category, which was more of an issue in 2010 than it is today. The novel is kind of paranormal fantasy, kind of historical fiction, kind of romantic, and kind of literary fiction. One agent said she liked the story, but vampires weren't selling, which was odd since this was the height of *Twilight* fever, *True Blood*, and *The Vampire Diaries*, among other popular blood-sucking tales. Maybe that was her way of saying she didn't like *Her Dear & Loving Husband*. I certainly don't know.

I had tried to find literary agents for previous projects and succeeded twice, with limited success. At the time, I felt like the problem was my writing. I wasn't good enough. My stories aren't compelling enough. You know, all the things writers say to themselves when feelings of impostor syndrome arise. But things were different with *Her Dear & Loving Husband*. I felt in my gut that there was an audience for James and Sarah Wentworth's story. Instead of becoming depressed, I was determined to find the audience I knew existed. Taking Bellows' lead, I trusted my own judgment, said to hell with you, and found my own readers, thousands of them, all over the world.

How do we avoid disillusion from rejection? By working hard over many years and learning to trust that we're good writers who create stories people want to read. Learn your strengths and your weaknesses, lean into your strengths, and improve your weaknesses. Believe in your abilities and trust your judgment. If you're submitting your work to agents or literary journals, don't let rejections wear you down. Keep submitting. Just as it takes time to learn how to write, it takes time to find the right home for your work.

Negative book reviews can also make writers feel like someone stabbed them in the heart. When it comes to reviews of my books, I have an easy way to handle them. I don't read them. You read that correctly. I don't read reviews of my work. I don't argue with anyone's right to dislike my work, and I don't argue with anyone's right to share their dislike. I certainly don't like every book I read, and I don't finish every book I begin. As an author, I have the right to choose what kind of energy I take in, and I choose to surround myself with positive energy that supports my vision. Yes, I know...woo-woo again. Let me try to be more practical.

First of all, negative reviews aren't the horrible thing they are made out to be. There's truth to the adage that there's no such thing as bad publicity. I think the *Fifty Shades of Grey* phenomenon some years ago is a great example. I had never seen a book with so many negative reviews (there are thousands of them), and yet it became one of the best-selling books of all time. If anything, the negativity fueled the phenomenon rather than quelled it since it made people curious. There was a time when writers were told that negative reviews were the kiss of death for their books, and maybe some people still believe that, but I've seen books sell well after many negative reviews.

It's not only the number of reviews you have but the type of reviews. Not all reviews are created equal. A five-star review that says "Great Book!" is okay, but a five-star review where readers go into some detail about why they liked the book can be helpful. It's the same with one-star reviews. One-star reviews where readers state why they didn't like the book are fine. Really, they're fine. It's not realistic to expect that everyone who reads your book will like it. People have different tastes, that's all. Then, there are the one-star reviews that come from a desire to be snarky toward the book or the author. I trust the intelligence of readers, and I believe they can tell the difference between honest reviews and mean-spirited reviews. They can tell if someone is simply sharing their dislike of a book or being mean for the fun of it. And don't forget those entertaining reviews that comment on the timeliness of the shipping or the condition of the product. The other day, I was scanning the reviews for a book I wanted to buy and there was a one-star review because the book arrived in four days instead of two. I bought the book, in case you were wondering.

I understand why writers feel hurt when their work is turned down by a literary agent or a journal or when they read criticism of their book. I received my fair share of rejection letters over more than 20 years. I used to be hypersensitive to such criticism. Creative writing classes at university were hard for me since there was an unnecessary sting in the feedback from other students. I thought the point of the writers' workshop was to help each other, not hurt each other. I didn't understand the meanness in the other students' critiques, and I didn't find those classes useful. When I began *The Copperfield Review* in 2000, I received some anonymous emails that put down the stories *Copperfield* published. I guessed at the time that the emails were from a writer I didn't publish, but I was new enough in the game that I found the comments hurtful. In time, I learned to set such nonsense aside and focus on what I loved about running the journal.

When *Her Dear & Loving Husband* was published in 2011, I was known by exactly zero people. At first, I read every review that popped up because I was fascinated by these strangers who took the time to say things about my book. After a while, though, I realized that the reviews—both good and bad—weren't entirely about my book. I know that sounds odd, but I believe that reviews have more to do with the reviewer than the book being reviewed. If you give two people the same book and one loves it and one hates it, is that about the book or the people reading the book?

When we read, all we have is our unique point of view as a lens through which to understand the story. We have our personalities, our perspectives, our likes, our dislikes, our interests, our emotions, our imaginations, and all of those traits come into play when we read. Sometimes that works in the writer's favor and sometimes it doesn't. Besides, a book for sale on Amazon, for example, with only stellar reviews will look fishy to readers since all books have some negative reviews. Take a moment to look up reviews of your favorite books and notice the one-star reviews. As long as more people like your book than dislike it, all is well.

It's the same with a "no" from a literary journal. Editor 1 might pass on your story, and maybe even Editors 2, 3, and 4. Editor 5 thinks the story is okay but maybe it needs a rewrite. Finally, Editor 6 (or Editor 11, 24, or 36) thinks it's the best thing ever exactly as is. If you stopped submitting after Editor 4, you never would have found the right home for your work. If you hadn't trusted your vision for your story, you might have taken Editor 5's suggestions for revisions when Editor 10 thought the story was perfect as it was. I want to stress the fact that I don't mean that our stories are always 100% correct the way we write them. It's always helpful to get feedback from writers and editors we trust. But if someone is telling you to rewrite your story in a way that doesn't fit your vision, that's something to be aware of.

If someone is writing an honest review or giving honest feedback and they didn't like your work, it's okay. I promise —both you and your work will be fine. It just means that person isn't meant to be your reader. Focus on the readers who like what you do. They're the ones who are going to buy your books.

If you're embracing the writing life, you need a lot of fortitude. A creative life is not for the faint of heart. We need thick skins. Keep writing and submitting, and in time you'll discover your path. Being a writer boils down to trust. Trusting yourself, your talent, your vision, and trusting that in time your work will begin to connect with the readers who love what you do.

23

WHAT A WRITING BOOK CAN'T TEACH YOU

What is the biggest obstacle to creativity? Attachment to outcome. As soon as you become attached to a specific outcome, you feel compelled to control and manipulate what you're doing and in the process you shut yourself off to other possibilities. Creativity isn't just about succeeding. It's about experimenting and discovering.

—Gordon MacKenzie

One of the things I love most about embracing the writing life is that there's no right way to do it. Every creative person, whether they're writers, sculptors, or painters, is an individual with their own beliefs, desires, and ways of being in the world. It's impossible to create a road map because each of us will be led in different directions by our unique natures.

Writers, especially new writers, want someone to tell them what to do and how to do it. There are ways to learn more about the art and craft of writing. We can look at examples from other writers. That's how we learn what good writing and not-so-good writing looks like. When I was a young university student, I would sit with Dickens, Morrison, and Whitman, spending hours handwriting their words into my notebooks. That's how I learned to put words, sentences, and ideas together. When I'm writing a novel, I read novels that are similar to what I'm trying to create for ideas and inspiration. My current work in progress is a murder mystery, so I've been reading mysteries galore. Reading other novels in the same genre adds so much to my creative well. Reading books about writing can be helpful as well. I've read many of them, believe me, especially when I was a fresh-faced writer dutifully taking my literature, screenwriting, and creative writing courses. I combed through those how-to writing books, searching for that road map, desperately seeking the magic formula that would allow me to write my own brilliant works.

My favorite writing books are the ones by Natalie Goldberg and Anne Lamott because they don't make declarations about how you *must* write. They are sharing their unique creative journeys. Stephen King does the same in *On Writing*. Okay, King makes declarations, but then he's Stephen King and he's allowed to make some declarations. But even King is clear about the fact that he's writing about his habits and preferences, and he points out that different writers will do things differently. Books like *On Writing*, *Writing Down the Bones*, and *Bird By Bird* are valuable because there's a lot to learn from seeing how other authors develop their habits and skills.

Even with all of the wonderful advice out there, there is still one thing that no writing book on earth can teach. Can you guess what it is? I'll give you a moment...

The one thing no writing book can teach is how to write.

That's right. No writing book, not one, can teach you how to write.

The only way anyone can learn to write is by writing. Writing is the only way you'll learn how to formulate a beginning, middle, and end of a story, whether that story is fiction or nonfiction. Writing is the only way you'll learn to create believable characters and worlds. Yes, you need to read too. As Stephen King said, "If you don't have time to read, you don't have the time (or the tools) to write. Simple as that." At a certain point, you need to put the books aside, pick up your pen, or sit at your computer, and write. There is no getting around this fact.

How-to writing books can only inspire. They can give tips and tricks. They can spark the imagination. But they cannot teach you how to write. In *Painting the Past*, I shared stories about how I write historical fiction because that's all I can do from this side of the computer screen. I can't tell you exactly what you need to do to write historical fiction because I don't know you. I don't know how you learn, what your interests are, or what your writing process is. I don't know what your research process will be. Maybe you don't know that yourself yet. I can't teach you how to think or how to process information. I can give tips for how to create voice, but I can't teach writers how to show voice because that can only come from the writer. Plus, we have different influences. I think Charles Dickens is awesome sauce. You might think Dickens sucks eggs. That's okay. That's why there's always room for new writers with new ideas.

Many writers want a blueprint for how to write, especially for fiction. They want someone to give them a plan, a formula to follow. First do Step A, then Step B, then Step C until your story is all shiny and pretty-like and ready for the *New York Times* bestseller list. When some writers read a how-to book that offers suggestions, because that's all any writing book can do, they feel like they were ripped off. Wait a minute. This book didn't teach me how to write a book! No, it didn't because it can't. What the how-to writing books are actually telling you is how that one particular writer writes books. You might find that information helpful or you might not. Some writers dig the Snowflake method for writing novels, for example. Such formulas make me want to pop my own eyes out with spoons. Which one of us is right? We both are because we have different ways of writing.

No matter how much actionable advice you find in a writing book, you're still going to have to figure out how to write by writing. As Natalie Goldberg said, "Writing does writing." We learn by jumping in and flailing about and trying this and trying that and trying the other thing until we find something that works. Then, when you find something that works, you'll do more of that.

Look to writing books for ideas, inspiration, and explorations into how other writers do what they do. Look to writing books for some actionable advice and takeaways that you can experiment with. Ultimately, you need to start writing and keep writing until you find your way. E.L. Doctorow said, "Writing is like driving at night in the fog. You can only see as far as your headlights, but you can make the whole trip that way." I know from experience that this is true. But unless we commit ourselves to taking that drive, at a slow speed, maneuvering around the detours, we'll never learn how to write the stories we want to share.

The secret to learning how to write a book is writing a book. That's it.

24

TUNING OUT DISTRACTIONS

Pardon my sanity in a world insane.
—Emily Dickinson

WITH EVERY TYPE of social media, gaming, news, streaming, and videos at our fingertips, it's no wonder so many people who would love to embrace the writing life say they don't have time. Many people would like to start a new hobby, whether it's writing, painting, hiking, exercising, or baking, but they find themselves drawn to social media instead, or they're news junkies, or they're gamers. We live vicariously through others who present another kind of life. Someone I know said that we're wasting our time watching videos of other people living their lives so that we can live by proxy. I would add that we're busy watching other people live their lives so that we don't have to take responsibility for living our own.

The good news is that there's nothing inherently bad about the internet, videos, or gaming. The internet has opened a world of opportunities for many creatives, including myself. I couldn't have created my own publishing company or started *The Copperfield Review*, which was an online literary journal, without the internet. And there's nothing wrong with watching a few videos or reading some blog posts. The problem comes in the form of addiction to social media, where we become obsessed with the images presented to us. We develop the "Grass is Always Greener" syndrome. If I lived in the country, my life would be perfect. If I lived in the city, my life would be perfect. If I had that juicer, my life would be perfect.

One of my favorite websites, Tiny Buddha, shared a quote from Steve Furtick: "The reason we struggle with insecurity is because we compare our behind-the-scenes with everyone else's highlight reel." According to Emily Holland of Tiny Buddha, "Unfortunately, social media provides us with numerous platforms that help to quickly trigger that unpleasant self-disdain. I found myself comparing all aspects of my life, both internal and external, to someone I had never met."

I've lost track of the times I've been at a restaurant with friends, our phones tucked away in our bags, while we watched those around us on their phones, ignoring the friends or family beside them, who were also on their phones. Recently, I was at an outdoor mall with my mother. We ordered our coffees and sat at a table near the fountains where some small children splashed in the water. Most of the parents were fully present with their children, playing and splashing too. A few pulled out their phones, snapped a few pictures, and put their phones away. As my mom and I watched the children play, I noticed one mother as her small son ran through the fountains by himself while she texted away. She didn't look up to see where he was. She didn't notice that he ran clear across the courtyard to the restaurants at the other end. Fortunately, he came back on his own, and, of course, his mom was still texting, not bothering to look up to greet him.

Then there was the time I went bowling, and a small boy, maybe about four, was bowling by himself while his mother was engrossed in her phone. The woman was so distracted she didn't realize that her son grabbed a bowling ball and walked across three lanes toward the pins. He was nearly hit when a bowler fell over to stop himself from releasing the ball so he wouldn't hurt the child. The mother, who finally realized what had happened, grabbed her son's hand and dragged him away as if it were his fault.

How can we help ourselves tune out the distractions so that we can concentrate on how we truly want to spend our time? The first thing we can do is to reduce our time on social media. For years, social media was considered the end-all-be-all of our lives. Everything we ate, did, and visited was posted on social media. Creatives may have felt the pull of social media more strongly because everyone—from writing gurus to agents to publishers—insisted that we had to create public platforms to get ourselves "out there," wherever "there" is. Writers have been told time and again that agents and publishers won't consider those who don't have a social media presence. Maybe one day it will dawn on someone that the person with the most followers doesn't win. It doesn't matter if one million people follow you if only 50 of them pay attention to your posts. There are so many issues with algorithms not showing our posts to those who follow us without paying to boost those posts. Besides, so many followers are fake bots that the number itself becomes irrelevant. Chuck Wendig, on his website terribleminds.com, said this about social media: "Once upon a time,

Googling something was a reliable way to learn about it, but now you'll likely find yourself on a raft floating on a sea of bad information. Social media has become the staging ground for all this shit (and also how, in part, it leeches into the groundwater of the rest of the internet), and as such, social media has started to fall apart like everything else."

Social media isn't the holy ground it once was, if it ever truly was. I've never been enamored with social media. For whatever reason, I never found it interesting or a good use of my time. I'd rather be writing or art journaling or watching the sunset. I dabbled with Twitter when it was still Twitter and didn't like the toxic environment. I deleted the app years ago and haven't thought about it since except to write this sentence. I have a Facebook author page that I log into maybe once a week. I "post and ghost," which is a fancy way of saying I add my blog posts to my feed and click out. I haven't logged into my Facebook Friend page for years. I enjoy watching a few YouTube videos now and then from creators I like, mostly of the BookTube variety, but I use that as a treat for myself at the end of the day after I'm finished with whatever I have to do. I've never had alerts on my phone for any reason because I find them annoying. I had an Instagram account that I used for one week before I deleted it. I check my email once a day. Other than that, emailers can wait. If Steven Spielberg emails me wanting to make movies of my books, he'll have to wait too.

If you're more involved in social media than I am, give yourself a limited amount of time each day in which to scroll through your feeds and add content. If you're mindlessly scrolling just to see if there's something new that wasn't there ten minutes ago, redirect your attention and see if there's something else you can do with your time. Even if you write one hundred words of your book during the time you would have spent scrolling, writing is always a better use of your time. You could also spend the odd ten minutes or so reading. Reading a good book is as good as it gets. Since I'm not worried about social media, I have time to write, bake, cook, color, do yoga, and enjoy my patio oasis with my little garden of potted plants. I'd much rather sit there and enjoy the blue sky than stare at my phone as if it's the only thing worthwhile. If we focus on what is truly important, and if we've decided that writing belongs under that category of importance, then we have more time to embrace the creativity that makes us feel alive.

With social media, compare-itis rears its head once again. A few years ago I would check my book sales several times a day. When I was active on social media, the little I used it even then, I constantly checked my followers, likes, and shares. No matter how many books I sold, it was never enough. Instead of being proud of my accomplishments, I continued to compare myself to others and I felt like a failure. Thich Nhat Hanh said, "If you feel your dreams aren't coming true, you might think that you need to do more, or think or strategize more. In fact, what you might need is less —less noise coming to you from both inside and outside— so that you have the space for your heart's truest intention to germinate and flourish." By giving up the compare-itis, by allowing myself the peace of accepting my creative world as it is—slow, quiet, and right for me—suddenly, overnight it seemed, my life became more peaceful. I'm more content with where I am at this moment.

We don't need to stay away from the internet. Still, we should be aware of how we use it. Content that challenges us to consider the world differently, content that improves our lives (I've found many wonderful Buddhist teachers who share lessons in mindfulness that have helped me), and content that assists us with our hobbies (I love learning about art journaling, crocheting, cooking, and baking) can be wonderful. But then, and here's the important part, we should take what we learn and put it into practice. As I continue to learn more about mindfulness, I set aside time every day to meditate, usually at the end of the day when the house is quiet. Putting what I learn into practice applies to everything I do. When I learn a new crochet stitch, I use it in my next project. I've discovered recipes that I've used many times. Watching someone bake just for the sake of watching someone bake doesn't improve my life. Except for *The Great British Bake Off*. I watch *Bake Off* just for the sake of watching *Bake Off*.

It's fine to admire beautiful photography and videography, and it's fine to admire nature scenes and scrumptious-looking scones. But we cannot forget to live our own lives, as imperfect and vulnerable as we are in our messy humanness. Seeking answers outside of ourselves will never work. Besides, the answers are already there, inside us, if we're brave enough to look. We need to be the best we can be in this moment and ask no more of ourselves. We need to be mindful of how we spend our time. And if we're writers, then we need to make time for writing.

25

THE COURAGE TO LET OUR LIGHT SHINE

Our deepest fear is not that we are inadequate. Our deepest fear is that we are powerful beyond measure. It is our light, not our darkness that most frightens us. We ask ourselves, Who am I to be brilliant, gorgeous, talented, fabulous? Actually, who are you not to be? You are a child of God. Your playing small does not serve the world. There is nothing enlightened about shrinking so that other people won't feel insecure around you.

—Marianne Williamson

One thing that most writers, or most creatives, have to come to terms with is the fact that others are not always happy for us when good things happen. The above quote from Williamson speaks to something I've struggled with throughout the years—the part that feels like I should dim my light because I might make other people uncomfortable while I stayed true to my calling as a writer.

My guess, based on my own experience, is that some people feel as if other people's accomplishments are a reflection of them somehow. I've had the “Who does she think she is?” response more times than I can count. Once, a friend at work was happy for me when a local magazine featured an article about my writing. She posted a link to the article on our work message board. As soon as I saw her post, I thought, “Oh no. This isn't going to be good.” I knew from previous experience that other people's reactions would not be positive. After my friend posted the link, a few people went to her with the old “Who does she think she is?” line. When some of them started the "Who do you think you are?" with me, I said that whatever I've achieved it's because I've worked hard. Was that the right response? I certainly don't know. Writing is how I choose to spend my free time. When I was addressing the naysayers, I felt like I should explain away the fact that I received attention for my writing so others would know that I don't think I'm “all that.” I work hard at certain pursuits, and as a result, sometimes good things happen. My accomplishments don't negate anyone else's accomplishments. There isn't a limited amount of success in this world.

There have been times when I've slunk around, my head hung low, avoiding eye contact with anyone. Then, in moments of clarity, I ask myself why I'm hiding away. The “Who does she think she is?” issue becomes a problem when we seek external acknowledgment or validation. Once we recognize that we don't need anyone else's approval, we're free from the labels others want to thrust upon us. If others disapprove, they are allowed to have their opinions. But we don't have to accept their opinions as our own. Rabbi Alan Lew said, “Quite often people's negative responses to us are rooted in their own twisted psychologies and not in anything we have done or said to provoke them.”

There's an episode of Jay Shetty's podcast *On Purpose*

With Jay Shetty called "Four Reasons We Crave External Validation." Shetty said that when we have a more grounded and supported sense of who we are, we are more likely to have an accurate understanding of ourselves. We have a stronger sense of self, and therefore we are less likely to be swayed by the opinions of others. Shetty used the example of Bruce Lee, who came to a similar conclusion while he was filming *The Green Hornet*. Lee realized that he was acting like a robot, trying to gain external validation by moving and speaking the way he thought he was expected to instead of the way he normally would. From that experience, Lee learned the importance of being yourself and not imitating others.

According to Shetty's blog, "You don't have to defend who you are in this world. You are not responsible for what others think of you. Your responsibility is to live in a way that adheres to your values and priorities. You can use input from others to help calibrate your thoughts and actions but do not rely on them for your sense of self."

What is it exactly that others mind about our being writers? It's hard to say precisely because the issue is likely different for each person. I've discovered that many people have left their dreams by the wayside with a myriad of excuses about why they can't...why they can't... Those of us who pursue our art despite the difficulties become highly frowned upon alien-like beings. We are the outliers, which is good for us but perhaps not so good for others.

I've lost track of how many people have said to me, "I'd love to write, but I have a full-time job." So do I. So do many other writers. Others have said to me, "I'd love to write, but I don't have a lot of time." Most writers struggle with finding time to write, but they get their writing done anyway. When someone says to me that they're a writer, I always ask what they're writing and often they don't have an answer. They *want* to write, which is different than *writing*. Perhaps for that reason, when someone sees that I do write, that I've published 14 books over 13 years, I suddenly become someone to be wary of. As Chuck Wendig said, "You are going to meet many people in your life who will not take your writing seriously. I wish this weren't so. Sometimes the people who won't take it seriously will be some of the most important people in your life—friends, loved ones, coworkers." I've experienced this too many times to count. Somehow, I was born into a family of people who have never read a book in their lives. I know for a fact they haven't read a single book I've published. Others, taking that Carly Simon song to heart (*You're so vain, I bet you think this song is about you...*), search everything I write for something of themselves.

There are wonderful things about life as a creative person. For me, the positives of being a writer far outweigh the negatives. I could say the tittering of others was so bad at times that it stopped me from writing, but it never did. Not once. In truth, it's not so hard to deal with the nitpickers and the naysayers. I prefer to focus on things I can control, and while I can't control other people's reactions to my creative life, I can control my reactions to other people. For those who insist on being negative about my writing, I ignore them. They don't like the fact that I'm a writer? So what? Their opinions are just that—their opinions—but I have my own life to lead, and my life includes writing. To get past the noise, because that's all the naysayers are—noise—I still my mind, focus on what I'm doing and remember the joy that writing brings me.

Brené Brown said that we should only share our stories with those who deserve to hear them. Brown also said, in one of my all-time favorite quotes, "Don't try to win over the haters. You are not a jackass whisperer." From experience, I know that to be true. Friends, people I know I can trust, hear my stories about the ups and downs of being a creative person, and they are the only ones who need to hear those stories. The friends I talk to about writing are writers and creators themselves, so they understand the idiosyncracies of an artistic calling.

When you are a writer and you stay stubbornly true to your calling, good things will happen. It might take time, but you'll finish your first book, you'll be published in some format, and you'll share your work with the world. Maybe you'll win awards. Maybe you'll sell a lot of books. Hold onto everything good about each step of the journey. You are working toward achieving your goals, and you deserve every bit of goodness that comes your way. Don't let those with smaller minds take that away from you. Not ever.

26

ADVICE ON HOW TO BE HAPPY

I was waiting for my drink in a coffee shop when I saw this list from Robert Louis Stevenson (*Treasure Island*, *Kidnapped*, and *The Strange Case of Dr. Jekyll and Mr. Hyde*) pinned to the community board. His advice is as appropriate today as it was over one hundred years ago. Stevenson said in 12 steps what it took me an entire book to say. But that's why he's Robert Louis Stevenson.

1. Make up your mind to be happy. Learn to find pleasure in simple things.

2. Make the best of your circumstances. No one has everything, and everyone has something of sorrow intermingled with gladness of life. The trick is to make the laughter outweigh the tears.

3. Don't take yourself too seriously. Don't think that somehow you should be protected from misfortune that befalls other people.

4. You can't please everybody. Don't let criticism worry you.

5. Don't let your neighbor set your standards. Be yourself.

6. Do the things you enjoy doing but stay out of debt.

7. Never borrow trouble. Imaginary things are harder to bear than real ones.

8. Since hate poisons the soul, do not cherish jealousy, enmity, grudges. Avoid people who make you unhappy.

9. Have many interests. If you can't travel, read about new places.

10. Don't hold post-mortems. Don't spend your time brooding over sorrows or mistakes. Don't be one who never gets over things.

11. Do what you can for those less fortunate than yourself.

12. Keep busy at something. A busy person never has time to be unhappy.

27

IN CONCLUSION

Don't quit. It's very easy to quit during the first ten years. Nobody cares if you write or not, and it's very hard to write when nobody cares one way or another. You can't get fired if you don't write, and most of the time you don't get rewarded if you do. But don't quit.

—Andre Dubus II

I HOPE that you've found something useful in this odd little book. Even after working on it for more than a year, I'm still not entirely sure what this book is supposed to be except possibly helpful for other writers dealing with the same issues I've struggled with for years.

I wanted to share how much being a writer feeds my soul. I wanted to share what I've learned about embracing the writing life, and I wanted to share some of the aspects of the creative life that aren't talked about enough. I wanted to say something about what it means to have courage, take your stand, and stay true to who you are even when it seems to be at odds with family or societal expectations. I wanted to share how writing has saved my life on more than one occasion. Perhaps through the lessons I've learned the hard way, you can see a way through to embracing a writing life of your own.

I challenge everyone interested in embracing the writing life to be open to new ideas, or at least the same ideas expressed in different ways. That is the essence of writing—looking at the world through the eyes of a child, as though everything is fascinating and new, and then sharing your newfound awareness, those unique observations that only could have come from you, with the world. When the writing is good, lean into it. There is nothing better than when words and ideas flow so smoothly that we struggle to keep up. When the writing is slower, and it will be, know that this too shall pass. I've dealt with burnout on and off for more than two decades, and always my love for writing sees me through.

I hope it will do the same for you.

AUTHOR'S NOTES

As always, I express my deepest gratitude to my readers from all over the world.

Thank you to the readers who follow me on my blog, some of them for more than a decade. A few of these chapters began life as blog posts. The posts have been updated, fleshed out, and given new life.

Here are the books that helped me write this book. I hope you'll find as much inspiration from them as I have.

Zen and the Art of Writing by Ray Bradbury

The Artist's Way by Julia Cameron

Big Magic by Elizabeth Gilbert

Writing Down the Bones, *Wild Mind*, and *Writing On Empty* by Natalie Goldberg

Silence by Thich Nhat Hanh

On Writing by Stephen King

Bird By Bird by Anne Lamott

This is Real and You Are Completely Unprepared by Rabbi Alan Lew

The War of Art and *Turning Pro* by Steven Pressfield

The Creative Act by Rick Rubin
Gentle Writing Advice by Chuck Wendig

ABOUT THE AUTHOR

Meredith Allard is an award-winning author known for the bestselling *Loving Husband Trilogy* and the Victorian novel *When It Rained at Hembry Castle*, which IndieReader named a Best Historical Novel. Her prequel, *Down Salem Way*, earned the B.R.A.G. Medallion and was a semi-finalist for the Chaucer Award in Early Historical Fiction.

A recognized authority on the craft, Meredith is the author of *Painting the Past: A Guide for Writing Historical Fiction*, a #1 Amazon New Release in Authorship and Creativity Self-Help. For over twenty years, she has mentored writers of all ages, helping them find their voices while honing her own signature blend of meticulous research and haunting prose.

When she isn't unearthing the secrets of the past, she can be found in the hills of Southern Nevada with her cats and a cup of coffee.

Join Meredith online at www.meredithallard.com for her weekly blog posts and monthly newsletter.

BOOKS BY MEREDITH ALLARD

And Shadows Will Fall

Christmas at Hembry Castle

Down Salem Way

The Duchess of Idaho

Her Dear & Loving Husband

Her Loving Husband's Curse

Her Loving Husband's Return

Painting the Past: A Guide for Writing Historical Fiction

The Professor of Eventide

The Swirl and Swing of Words: Embracing the Writing Life

Victory Garden

When It Rained at Hembry Castle

Woman of Stones

www.ingramcontent.com/pod-product-compliance
Lightning Source LLC
LaVergne TN
LVHW090611110826
845146LV00001B/340

* 9 7 9 8 2 1 8 5 4 0 2 9 6 *